THE STUDY OF THEOLOGY

Foundations of Contemporary Interpretation
Moisés Silva, Series Editor
Volume 7

THE STUDY OF THEOLOGY

From Biblical Interpretation to Contemporary Formulation

Richard A. Muller

ZondervanPublishingHouse
Academic and Professional Books
A Division of HarperCollins*Publishers*
Grand Rapids, Michigan

ACADEMIE BOOKS is an imprint of Zondervan Publishing House
1415 Lake Drive, S.E., Grand Rapids, Michigan 49506.

Library of Congress Cataloging in Publication Data

Muller, Richard A. (Richard Alfred). 1948–
    The study of theology : from biblical interpretation to
contemporary formulation /
Richard A. Muller.
        p.   cm. – (Foundations of contemporary interpretation ; v. 7)
    Includes bibliographical references and index.
    ISBN 0-310-41001-0
    1. Theology.   I. Title.   II. Series.
BR118.M83   1991
230'.01–dc20   90-39919
                                                                CIP

2876474

Edited by Gerard Terpstra and Leonard G. Goss
Designed by Louise Bauer

Printed in the United States of America

91 92 93 94 95 96 / CH / 10 9 8 7 6 5 4 3 2

CONTENTS

EDITOR'S PREFACE

"Interpretation does not end with exegesis" (see below, p.xi). With that understatement, Professor Muller alerts us to the great breadth of theological perspective that should inform our reading of Scripture.

As I sought to point out in the first volume of this series, much biblical scholarship has overreacted to the danger—a real danger to be sure—of allowing theological commitments to impose a predetermined meaning on the text (see *Has the Church Misread the Bible?* pp. 19–23). This overreaction has led many interpreters to ignore the intimate connection that exists between exegesis and the other theological disciplines. In his defense of the classical fourfold model (the biblical, historical, systematic, and practical disciplines), Professor Muller broadens the reader's horizons and brings in a much-needed corrective.

What also comes through in his exposition, however, is that (in a somewhat different sense) interpretation does not *begin* with exegesis either. Biblical scholars who downplay the significance of theology for exegesis only fool themselves if they think they can approach the text without theological predispositions. And the best antidote for the *unconscious* , and often detrimental, intrusion of such assumptions is to develop a coherent understanding of the way theology functions in the hermeneutical process.

Professor Muller proves himself a capable guide for doing just that. He is one of those rare scholars who have managed to combine deep specialization in a chosen field with breadth of erudition. A recognized authority in the area of post-Reformation dogmatics, he has however also written on a wide variety of theological topics. Accordingly, he demands some effort and concentration on the part of the reader. Biblical students with little prior interest in theology may be tempted to balk. They will be the poorer if they give in to that temptation. Cutting corners seldom works in hermeneutics.

The author acknowledges the controversial character of many of the issues he discusses. His primary aim, however, is not to persuade us about a particular way of solving the problems, but to understand the nature of those problems. Whether we agree or disagree with him, he wants us to do so consciously and intelligently. I commend this volume as a signal contribution to the all-important task of integrating hermeneutics into the whole theological enterprise.

Moisés Silva

INTRODUCTION

A middle-aged and much-experienced minister stood before the graduating class, faculty, and guests at the commencement exercises of a well-known American seminary. He had been called upon to speak as a representative new graduate of one of the more popular degree programs, the Doctor of Ministry. Dressed in his new robe and elegant doctoral hood, he mounted the podium with words of praise for the seminary, words that, by his own admission, were as much a surprise to himself as to anyone else. He had always frowned on seminaries and seminary education. He had warned dozens of young people about the "ivory tower" of academic study and its irrelevance to the "real work" of ministry. He had mocked processes of accreditation that only resulted in making seminaries more academic and more isolated from reality. He had scorned the theological speculations that led away from and undermined the faith. Why, then, was he graduating from a seminary? He was there because of the practical, "how-to" approach of the Doctor of Ministry degree. He was there because this degree was different—it demanded no theological speculation, no academic, ivory-tower critical thinking, no retreat from the nitty-gritty reality of daily ministry. In fact, the ivory-tower courses—courses dealing with critical exegesis, the history of Christian doctrine, and philosophical and systematic theology—had not been a part of his program of education. He had studied only useful, relevant subjects.

The speaker didn't see me wince. Nor did he see me shake my head somewhat sadly over what appeared to me to be his failure to see the crucial interrelationship of the task of ministry and the work of theology. He couldn't see me because I was behind him on the platform sitting quietly with the other benighted residents of the ivory tower. This new graduate, dressed in the splendid new robes of his new degree, I noted to myself, was taking nothing home with him but his diploma and his hood. He had come and gone and remained inwardly unchanged. He was quite pleased with himself and quite representative not only of a certain constituency in any graduating class of almost any seminary but also of a deep problem in the study of theology in America. Theology made no sense to him. He was intent on practicing ministry without it. Where had he gone wrong? Where had *we* gone wrong?

Perhaps what was most disturbing to me was that my own teaching career in seminary had been preceded by seven years of parish ministry, three as an assistant in a fairly large urban church and four as the sole minister in a small rural church, and I had come to the task of teaching with a firm conviction that everything I had learned both in seminary and in graduate school had been of use to me in my ministry. I firmly believed and still do believe that the year-long sequence that I teach on the history of Christian doctrine does relate directly to the concerns of ministry. When I taught systematic theology, I operated under the same conviction. And I hold a similar conviction for the courses in Old and New Testament— including the courses that deal with critical, textual problems— taught by my colleagues in those fields. On the one hand, I was somewhat relieved that our new Doctor of Ministry had taken no courses in historical, systematic, or biblical theology at our seminary: at least his remarks had been made in ignorance of our course offerings in those areas. On the other hand, I was filled with deep worries over the nature of his studies and over his failure to recognize the importance not merely of theological study but also of thinking theologically.

What is the connection between the interpretive study of Scripture and the other fields of study emphasized in seminary training and in Christian ministry? How do the results of our exegesis of Scripture impinge on our reading and understanding of the history of the church and its doctrines, on our study and use of systematic theology, on our apologetics or defense of the faith, and on the widely varied areas of ministerial practice and Christian life? From one point of view, the answers to these questions ought to be self-evident. If the Reformation battle cry of *sola Scriptura* still echoes at the heart of Protestantism, then the interpretation of Scripture must be the foundation of our evaluation and use of the materials of historical and systematic theology and the firm basis of all preaching, counseling, and Christian living. We should not even need to ask the questions.

The questions, however, do press upon us constantly and consistently, particularly because the interpretive problems recognized by most contemporary theologians and felt, albeit uncomprehendingly, by our graduation speaker render the movement from biblical text to doctrinal formulation considerably more difficult today than in the sixteenth century. The traditional forms of theology and preaching frequently fail the tests of exegesis and contemporary theologizing—while, at the same time, much contemporary theology and exegesis fails to address directly the needs of the church.

How often do we hear quaint moralizing or amateurish psychologizing instead of biblical, exegetical, or expository preaching? Even the best of preachers experience at times the feeling that direct address of contemporary problems sometimes calls for a less-than-traditional sermon, and that such sermons move away from the time-honored exegetical and expository forms. How often do we hear the complaint (or experience it ourselves) that a particular doctrine or confession or system, whether it be the doctrine of the divine attributes or of the Trinity or of penal substitutionary atonement, does not easily fit into the modern practice of Christianity—perhaps because it is difficult to document directly from any single text of Scripture properly interpreted according to modern critical standards or perhaps because it seems impossible to correlate with any experience of life in our world? The most confessionally orthodox of teachers and preachers experience such worries, and those less content with the traditional forms of theology often find themselves at odds with the confessions of their church and divorced from the biblical message in its ancient context.

The problems illustrated by the speech at a seminary graduation cannot be dismissed as an individual aberration. They reach much deeper. They are the result of severance of theory from practice and practice from theory that has made many theological theoreticians question the intellectual and spiritual future of the church at large and the academic future of their disciplines—and that has led many ministerial practitioners to doubt the value of all things theological. But there ought to be no theology divorced from the practice of religion and no practice of religion without some theological consciousness of the meaning of its activity and work. Theological training as a whole—biblical, historical, and systematic, as well as "practical" or ministerial—ought to reflect the life of the church and be of value to the life of the church. Theological training, in short, ought to cohere. The basic, churchly meditation on Scripture ought, as it has in the past, to issue in a theology relevant to Christian life and practice.

There is, in other words, an intellectual and spiritual short circuit or, more accurately, a series of short circuits, that occur at some point between the study of Scripture and of the various other foundational disciplines in theology and the practice of preaching, teaching or counseling, the churchly work that ought to move forward on the basis of the church's theology. We have evidence of these short circuits in the remarks of the graduate, but we also have evidence of them in the frequently heard complaints that critical, historical exegesis does not lead to preaching, that theological system fails to address even indirectly either the problems identified by a critical exegesis of the text or by a life of ministry in the church, that the historical study of Christianity functions more as a display of museum-pieces than as a discovery of materials useful to us in our present. The graduating student had a problem, but he was not alone in it. The problem stands at the heart of theological study in the present day.

This book has grown out of a reflection on the needs and problems confronting theology in our time. Theology suffers from a lack of direction and a loss of unity among its subdisciplines. Exegesis and theological system, in particular, do not seem to function as part of a larger interpretive unity. This is, moreover, a problem that is not confined to students. The problem exists also among professionals, trained in the disciplines and charged with the task of teaching theology. We teach at a high level of sophistication, frequently with little or no concern for the way in which our subject contributes to the work of our colleagues or how the work of the entire theological faculty fits together into a greater whole for the service of Christian ministry. Several authors have come forward to demand the wholesale reappraisal of theological curriculum. There is a widespread doubt concerning the continued viability of the classical "fourfold" curriculum. And colleagues criticize what they call the "university model" of seminary education based on departmental units representing the four "classical" divisions of theological study.

I do not claim to find a definitive answer to these problems for all sectors of the theological community. I hope only to discuss the interpretive or hermeneutical implications of the fourfold curriculum—biblical, historical, systematic, and practical theology—to present a case for its structure, and to argue the essential unity of the disciplines in their service to the church. My hope, in other words, is to show that the biblical, historical, systematic, practical model is an interpretive structure that leads from the exegetical disciplines to theological formulation. There is, and there must be, a hermeneutical enterprise that is larger than the interpretive ventures of each of the various theological disciplines. Interpretation does not end with exegesis. The point of interpretation is not simply to show where an author is "coming from" but where the teachings of the author point. If, moreover, the teachings of biblical authors point authoritatively into our present, then our interpretive task leads far beyond the fundamental exegetical inquiry into the meaning of a text in its original context. Our interpretive task extends from the text, via the various disciplines that show the path of the text and its meaning into the present, to contemporary formulation.

The seeming dual emphasis of the present volume, therefore, is really a single emphasis, approached by way of two descriptions of its form. The emphasis falls on interpretation, specifically on patterns of interpretation larger than the initial address to a text. Formally, that emphasis can be described in terms of hermeneutics and "hermeneutical circles" (chapter 4) and in terms of the structure of biblical, historical, systematic, and practical study that should generate both the interest in interpretation and the proper context for address both to the authoritative text of Scripture and to the needs of the present-day community of faith.

My hope implies a rather ambitious venture. Were it not for the need, one might be tempted to consider it impossible and pass on to a highly specialized and therefore less troublesome exercise. My own attempt to teach what has been traditionally termed theological encyclopedia has only confirmed the difficulty of dealing, theoretically and schematically, with an entire curriculum. I am also impressed by the necessity of the task. If seminary study is to have any coherence and if it is to issue forth in coherent ministry, theology must make sense as a whole.

The contemporary critique of the fourfold curriculum, particularly as represented by the work of Edward Farley, contains some very important criticisms and insights, and any discussion of the study of theology and of the unity of "biblical, historical, systematic, and practical theology" must take them into consideration together with the works on theological study and formulation by Ebeling and Pannenberg. The second, related issue—the complaint against the "university model"—also needs to be discussed, albeit more briefly. The educational model found in our seminaries is not and never was a pure university model but rather a churchly model developed in recognition of the need of clergy to engage not simply in ministry but in *educated ministry*. The content and methods of the biblical, historical, and systematic disciplines, as traditionally taught in our seminaries, have rested on an assumption of a solid liberal arts education and have built on the liberal arts model, of course in a churchly direction. The complaint against the university model is, sadly, a complaint not unlike the complaint mounted against the classical liberal arts and social science curricula of our universities by the "forward looking" and incredibly mistaken educators of the mid-sixties and early seventies, who held that courses on Western Civilization and the Great Books could be replaced by "relevant" and "practical" courses.

Our situation is doubly sad, inasmuch as the seminary-based critics of the classical model have not learned from the disaster caused by their fellow-educators in the university. We have, in fact, encountered in our seminaries a problem identical to that examined in E. D. Hirsch's *Cultural Literacy* and Allan Bloom's *Closing of the American Mind*.[1] By looking away not only from the fourfold model for the study of theology but also from the traditional *content* of the fourfold model—instead of engaging in the admittedly difficult task of making the fourfold model work—seminaries have been guilty of creating several generations of clergy and teachers who are fundamentally ignorant of the materials of the theological task and prepared to argue (in their own defense) the irrelevance of classical study to the practical operation of ministry. The sad result has been the loss, in many places, of the central, cultural function of the church in the West and the replacement of a culturally and intellectually rich clergy with a group of practitioners and operations-directors who can do almost anything except make sense of the church's theological message in the contemporary context.

Making sense of the church's theological message in the contemporary context is really little more than the decisively Christian version of the great educational quest of the old liberal arts curriculum on which theology has rested since the foundation of the universities in the twelfth and thirteenth centuries. The issue has always been to understand and to be able to express our understanding of the world-order and of our place in it as human beings. The success of the great philosophers in

---

[1]E. D. Hirsch, Jr., *Cultural Literacy: What Every American Needs to Know* (New York: Houghton Mifflin, 1987); Allan Bloom, *The Closing of the American Mind: How Higher Education Has Failed Democracy and Impoverished the Souls of Today's Students* (New York: Simon & Schuster, 1987).

addressing that issue is what makes Plato and Aristotle still worth reading. And the success of such theologians as Aquinas, Luther, Calvin, and Schleiermacher in pressing the very same issue from the point of view of a theological or religious construction of reality is what makes their works crucial to the study of theology as it leads toward contemporary theological statement and to the task of ministry.

Beyond this fundamentally intellectual issue of the coherence of the message and of the ability of theology to address the deep concerns of world and culture, lies another, more subtle problem. As Hirsch and Bloom have recognized in their critiques of secular education,[2] the classical curricula did not only instill great ideas into young minds, they also instilled values along with the ideas. At a rather profound level, classical study built character. And as one colleague of mine has pointed out, the classical seminary education of the nineteenth and early twentieth centuries, like the classical university curriculum, was also profoundly concerned with building character.[3] It is a sad by-product of the loss of the older academic curricula that we also lie in danger of losing something not always noted in connection with intellectual growth: spiritual and moral fiber.

In my own experience in ministry, whether in a relatively large urban church or in a rural congregation, I was consistently impressed by the direct application to life, the immediate relevance, of my seminary training, particularly my training in the so-called classical disciplines, and even of my later graduate training in theology. I came from parish ministry to seminary teaching with the conviction, resting on the experience of day-to-day ministry, that biblical exegesis, church history, history of Christian doctrine, philosophy of religion, and doctrinal or dogmatic theology provided crucial resources for the everyday life of the believing community. Beyond this, the longer I worked in ministry, the stronger became my conviction that all

---

[2] Cf. Hirsch, *Cultural Literacy*, pp. 82–92, 98–102; Bloom, *Closing*, e.g., pp. 136–37.

[3] James E. Bradley, now engaged in work on the relationship of the building of character to seminary education in the U.S. under an ATS grant.

of my studies, despite their diversity (whether diversity of subject or diversity of approach as dictated by particular professors) functioned as an interpretive unity—and that theological thinking and Christian living were profoundly interrelated. To make the point in a somewhat different way: the theology I learned from my teachers in both the theoretical and the practical fields and the Christianity I both taught to and learned from the members of my two congregations are one and the same.

Finally, a word about the character and tone of this book: the themes and discussions I present are unabashedly theological and unabashedly systematizing. This does not mean that I intend for the study of theology or of any particular theological discipline to be conducted without any objectivity or without any examination of presuppositions. On the contrary, theological study is distinct from the generalized exercise of piety precisely because it is a self-conscious exercise that knows and examines its presuppositions, follows sound principles of analysis and interpretation, and consistently attempts to let its materials speak in terms of their own presuppositions and contents (particularly when some of those presuppositions and contents stand critically juxtaposed with the cherished assumptions of the present). Nonetheless the basic principles of analysis and interpretation recognize a fundamental connection between exegete and text, between the Christian and the Christian tradition, between the student of theology and all of his materials. Objectivity in analysis and commitment in faith need not be mutually exclusive.

All of the preceding considerations point to the fact that the theological pluralism of the present age is a barrier— perhaps an insurmountable one—to the creation of a single paradigm for the unified understanding and study of theology. No particular paradigm will be universally received. Granting this premise, the paradigm presented here has a certain specificity and restriction. I am unwilling, however, to adopt such classifications as "liberal" or "conservative," "rationalist" or "fideist" as characterizations either of what my position is or what it is not. Not only are these labels divisive, they are also misleading: when I read the theology of a "liberal" theologian of the early twentieth century, such as William Adams Brown or William Newton Clarke or even the somewhat notorious Charles Augustus Briggs, I come away with the distinct impression that none of these writers can easily be classified as "liberal" in terms of our present-day theological spectrum. I much prefer terms like "contemporary" or "contemporizing," "traditional," "historical perspective," "critically orthodox," or even a term like Oden's "post-modern orthodoxy"—although each of these is also far from perfect.

My underlying hope in writing this book is to present a view of theology that respects and preserves the truths and insights of the Christian tradition but that also points toward a way of understanding and stating those truths and insights in the contemporary context. In other words, the model proposed here for the study of theology attempts to be traditional but not locked into the past; orthodox in proposing a churchly "right teaching" but without attempting to repristinate a particular historical form of orthodoxy; historical and critical in its recognition of the character of our tradition and the tools necessary to its correct examination but not to the extent either of tearing down the edifice of the tradition or of turning it into a museum incapable of present-day relevance. In addition, the model is intended to be broadly and generally useful, granting that it provides a pattern for understanding the working of theology and the productive movement of study through the disciplines rather than a discussion of a particular theological system or the relationship of the various parts of theological study to such a system.

Since, moreover, this book is about the interpretive unity of the studies that spring historically and functionally from the biblical foundations of Christian faith, it is written at all points with a view toward that unity. Thus, the sections on biblical and historical study will contain references to the systematic and practical disciplines. Whereas I hope to stand firmly against the tendency to prejudge the biblical materials on the basis of the history of doctrine or contemporary dogmatics or contemporary praxis, I find myself totally incapable of considering any one aspect of theological study or any one of the basic theological disciplines apart from its relationship to the others. It is precisely the development of a viable picture of those relationships that is the subject of this book.

I undertake this synthesizing approach fully aware that my own academic specialization stands in the way of the task and that the problem of the fragmentation of theology into isolated subdisciplines is a problem in which I participate and, to the extent that I teach in my own area of specialization to the exclusion of other areas, a problem of my own making. This book is a prospectus for overcoming the problem and the perception of fragmentation in the study of theology. I come to it as a historian of doctrine who also works in the area of systematic theology—so that I have a sense of the historically conceived unity of theological thinking and some hope for present-day synthesis. My weaknesses, apart from those inherent in my own specialized work, will surely lie in the other areas touched on by this volume. I especially ask the forgiveness of colleagues in the fields of Old and New Testament study, where I am a dabbler at best—but I also hope that my attempt here at forming an overarching prospectus for unified study and interpretation of theology will provide both help and stimulation to teachers and students, to concerned clergy and laity who feel the need for such an effort as strongly as I do.

1

THE STUDY OF THEOLOGY: ISSUES AND PROBLEMS

PRELIMINARY ASSUMPTIONS

The study of theology has never been an easy task. Writers in past ages of the church—from the age of the fathers, to the high scholastic era of the thirteenth and fourteenth centuries, to the era of Reformation and post-Reformation Protestantism—have declared with a notable uniformity that the study of theology calls for a complete devotion on the part of the student. They were convinced that it demands a mastery of tools and sources, a grasp of language and philosophy, and an openness to, indeed, a desire for inward, spiritual formation and development. Christian thinkers have always recognized, moreover, the difficulty of moving from the text of Scripture into the church's present with a doctrine and a preaching relevant to the concerns of Christian congregations and Christian missions. Nevertheless, despite these difficulties, the church in past ages was remarkably successful in its work. Methods of interpretation, credal formulations, overarching systematic expressions of the faith, and architectonic consideration of the interrelationship of the several disciplines and subdisciplines in theology have, in these past ages, proved capable of opening the text of Scripture and bringing the Word to bear doctrinally and practically on the life of the church.[1]

When we survey the contemporary state of theology, however, a different picture emerges. We see profound debate over methods of interpretation focused on the seemingly negative effects of the higher criticism on the doctrinal and practical work of Christian theology. We see a decay of interest in and commitment to old creeds and confessions without any corresponding interest in or commitment to the production of new creeds and confessions of a comparable biblical and doctrinal quality to those being quietly set aside. We detect no dearth of theological systems, but even a cursory examination of most of these productions reveals a failure to reflect concerns of the contemporary church and a certain intellectual and spiritual distance between dogmatic system and Christian piety or the Christian pulpit. Finally, we encounter a degree of curricular uncertainty among many Christian educators concerning the possibility of creating a cohesive model for the integration and churchly use of the disciplines and subdisciplines in the theological "encyclopedia."

Of course, not all of these problems are present everywhere in the life of church and seminary, nor are they felt with equal intensity. Some denominations still maintain a strong commitment to their creeds and confessions, and there are surely some seminaries and some individual theologians who are reasonably successful in overcoming the separation frequently noted between theological system and Christian life. The theological curriculum, moreover, ought to function as an organized body of teaching that is production-oriented. When we ask the question of the relationship of biblical studies to contemporary theological statement, we are in fact asking the question of theological study, a question that ought to be answered at a general and theoretical level by the theological curriculum in order that it can also be answered at a specific and

---

[1]Cf. Moisés Silva, *Has the Church Misread the Bible? Foundations of Contemporary Interpretation*, vol. 1 (Grand Rapids: Zondervan, 1987), especially chaps. 2 and 3.

concrete level by the individual practitioner whether teacher, clergy, or laity.

Much of the discussion about contemporary theology and theological education has focused on the standard division of theology into the biblical, historical, systematic, and practical fields, as inherited by our schools and seminaries from the teachers of the nineteenth century. The fourfold model appears to be a fairly objective description of the structure of theology until one examines the subdisciplines that fit rather uncomfortably at times under the rubrics of biblical, historical, systematic, and practical theology. These subdisciplines, at least as they are typically presented in the present day, exist as more or less isolated subject areas rather than as individual aspects of a larger whole cohering harmoniously in dialogue with one another. The problem is illustrated by a survey of the various topics in the curriculum and the problems encountered as we study these topics or subject areas.

The beginning theological student and the parish minister in our highly pluralistic society are both faced with a profound educational, spiritual, and intellectual problem, considerably greater and graver in scope and implication than that faced by theological students and clergy in past ages. That problem may be addressed, at least in part, from the point of view of the many and varied sources and perspectives that must be addressed by theology today. The modern era has brought about a proliferation of theological disciplines and subdisciplines. Theology today does not build, simply, as it did in the eleventh and twelfth centuries, on two clearly defined bodies of knowledge—Scripture and tradition. Nor can we, today, pronounce the solution of the Reformation—*sola Scriptura*, Scripture alone—with the simplicity and ease of the sixteenth century. We now face, not one tradition, but many traditions: denominational theologies, independent academic theologies, infinite numbers of "isms," and a growing number of restricted topical theologies, products of the religious version of the "political action committee" or private-interest lobby. This plethora of traditions and types of theology clouds the *sola Scriptura* of the Reformers, because any number of these

separate theologies—particularly the denominational and private-interest theologies—lay exclusive claim to biblical truth. If
one comes to theological study with a fairly open mind, the
problem of affiliation, alignment, and basic perspective will be
enormous.

For example, in studying systematic theology, you will
quickly come to realize that you are not studying systematic
theology as such but one of many variations of it. It will be
Reformed or Lutheran or Arminian or Roman Catholic systematic theology—or perhaps "evangelical" systematic theology,
although that label does not really identify the contents of a
system very closely. Or it might be an existentialist system like
Macquarrie's *Principles of Theology* or a "liberation" theology
like that of Gutiérrez or Segundo. In looking to biblical studies,
students will find a variety of approaches to the interpretation of
Scripture, ranging from a strict application of Hirsch's belief
that a text means essentially one thing, to a loose reading of a
theory like Gadamer's that would have a text mean different
things and point in several directions, all of them quite
correctly! Historical events and the progress of ideas are subject
to a variety of interpretations—and any honest historian will
point out that one always deals with interpretation and never
simple fact. As for the practical field, students and ministers will
find not only a wide array of topics but also an entire spectrum
of relationships to the other fields of study, including the rather
extreme opinion that identifies biblical, systematic, and historical studies as essentially theoretical and then demands that
theory take its point of departure from practice.

The diversification of theological curriculum presents a
similar problem. Whereas the theological student of earlier
times—from the rise of the cathedral schools in the eleventh
century down to the period of Protestant orthodoxy in the
seventeenth century—learned essentially a single discipline of
traditional exegetical-dogmatic theology, the modern theological student is called upon to study such diverse subjects as
exegesis; hermeneutics; systematic, philosophical, and apologetic theology; ethics; church history; history of doctrine;
homiletics; liturgics; counseling; marriage and family ministry;

and Christian formation. It is quite true that all of these topics were covered by the older theology—only then the package was neater and more unified. Since there was virtually only one pattern of biblical interpretation prior to the sixteenth century, and in the sixteenth century essentially two opposing models, hermeneutics or the science of interpretation was simply a presuppositional element in exegesis, the interpretation itself. And since the assumption was held by virtually all theologians of these earlier times that the interpretation of Scripture led directly to the doctrine of the church, with no underlying problematic disturbing the transition, exegesis and dogmatics (or systematic theology) were quite easily conjoined.

As for the other subdisciplines, it was formerly assumed that all systems of doctrine would have a certain philosophical component—philosophy being the humble handmaid of theology—and that ethics sprang directly from the biblical command with an occasional nod to Aristotle. Since the Ten Commandments could be virtually equated with natural law, the divergences between Scripture and Aristotle could be dealt with easily. The so-called practical or ministerial disciplines were not taught: homilies were simply popular elaborations on scriptural texts that were done, not taught; liturgics was the repetition of a tradition of great antiquity; counseling ministries and personal formation were essentially taken for granted as the necessary by-products of the exegetical and doctrinal study. Church history and history of doctrine were, until the late seventeenth century, simply the sense of tradition and of the chronology of debate that underlay doctrinal formulation—again, not separate disciplines.

Today, by way of contrast, these subjects do not fit together so neatly, and they have all become the discrete specialty areas of scholars. The vast body of literature in each area has made it impossible for anyone to be a truly competent generalist in theological study or to be a recognized specialist in more than one particular area. On the positive side, of course, specialization can mean the considerable refinement of any given subject area and a better grasp of its materials. But few theological students will even train to be specialists: ministry is by its very nature the work of a generalist who can understand Scripture and church, preach sermons, make sense out of Christian doctrine in discussion with laity, counsel with individuals, and function as an interpreter of reality in an increasingly pluralistic world.

All of this can be a bit daunting to students and to clergy, particularly when it has been spelled out in stark detail. The difficulty is enormous, particularly for anyone who hopes to find a coherent whole in seminary education today. But it is not insurmountable. Our fear of the problem ought not to deter us from the study—any more than Christian's increasing knowledge of the dangers on his pilgrim way ought to have ended his progress before he reached the goal of Mount Zion. We do need, more than ever in history, to meditate on our theological curriculum as we encounter it (rather than in retrospect) and to discover the relationships between its various elements—for the sake of consistent and unified Christian ministry and witness. We need, in short, to understand, to map out the territory of theological study.

That is precisely the purpose of the subject traditionally called theological encyclopedia. *Encyclopedia* is a term that has fallen on bad times. It is used, typically, to refer to works like the *Encyclopedia of Philosophy*, the *Schaff-Herzog Encyclopedia of Religious Knowledge*, the *World Book Encyclopedia* or *Columbia Desk Encyclopedia*. Etymologically, however, the word offers a broader meaning. It contains three Greek components: *en-cyclo-paideia*. *Paideia* means teaching and, thus, "encyclopedia" means a complete circle or circuit of teaching. "Theological Encyclopedia" indicates the complete circle of theological knowing, organized not alphabetically but in terms of the interrelationships of the several subject areas of theology.[2]

Thus Old and New Testament studies, whether historical, exegetical, or theological can be grouped together as "biblical theology." The history of the church, as distinct from the

---

[2]Cf. the discussion in Abraham Kuyper, *Principles of Sacred Theology*, trans. De Vries (New York: Scribner, 1898; repr. Grand Rapids: Baker, 1980), pp. 1–23.

history of God's people within the canon of Scripture, encompasses institutional and doctrinal histories plus such subdivisions as the history of piety or spirituality. In the realm of contemporary theological endeavor, we can distinguish, more or less precisely, between disciplines that relate principally to knowing, the "systematic," and disciplines that relate principally to doing, the "practical." Systematic thinking includes doctrinal theology (sometimes called "systematic theology"), philosophical theology, apologetics, and ethics—all of which attempt to provide coherent structures of knowledge based on a given set of problems or ideas. The "practical" field encompasses those areas that relate directly to churchly practice or "doing"—homiletics; liturgics, or worship; counseling; ministry; and the practice of personal and corporate piety, which can be called Christian formation.

This broadly defined clustering of disciplines into four basic categories—biblical, historical, systematic, and practical—is not simply a convenient pattern for study. It is also a pattern that was developed in the light of interpretive considerations and with a view toward the "organic" unity of the various forms of theological study, primarily by a group of teachers and scholars in the nineteenth century.[3] Granting the historical origins of the model, it is certainly a mistake to view it as precritical or uncritical—and an even graver mistake to ignore its hermeneutical significance and its implications not merely for the path of study but also for the path to theological

[3]Cf. Kuyper, *Principles*, pp. 17–20; and see Edward Farley, *Theologia: The Fragmentation and Unity of Theological Education* (Philadelphia: Fortress, 1983), for a recent survey and analysis of the problems confronting the study of theology. For extended discussion of the history of theological study, see Charles Augustus Briggs, *History of the Study of Theology*, 2 vols. (London: Duckworth, 1916); George R. Crooks and John F. Hurst, *Theological Encyclopedia and Methodology, on the Basis of Hagenbach*, new ed., rev. (New York: Hunt and Eaton, 1894); Yves Congar, *A History of Theology*, trans. Guthrie (Garden City: Doubleday, 1968); recent, but rather poorly conceived, is Gillian R. Evans, Alister McGrath, and Allan D. Galloway, *The Science of Theology* (Grand Rapids: Eerdmans, 1987); cf. my review in *Consensus: A Canadian Lutheran Journal of Theology*, 13,1 (Spring 1987), pp. 114–15.

formulation. There is clear evidence in the works of several nineteenth-century formulators of the fourfold model of theological study that they viewed it as a model for the integration, not so much of a myriad of diverse disciplines, but of distinct but nonetheless related patterns of theological understanding into a framework for the contemporary interpretation of Christian doctrine.[4] Rightly understood, the traditional encyclopedic approach to theology can provide a larger hermeneutical or interpretive structure for the movement from exegesis to contemporary formulation.

TOWARD A UNIFIED STUDY OF THEOLOGY

Virtually all of the writers who have examined the study of theology in recent times—most notably Gerhard Ebeling, Edward Farley, and Wolfhart Pannenberg[5]—have remarked on the diversity and general disarray of the subject. And virtually all have recognized that this diversity and disarray both undermine the credibility of theology in our time and render exceedingly difficult if not impossible the task of reintegrating the theological disciplines in such a way that they support a cohesive and cogent ministry of the gospel. Ebeling, Farley, and Pannenberg not only agree on this rather negative point, they also agree that this disunity and dispersion of theology arises from a crisis of understanding concerning theology that has its roots in the age of Enlightenment and the nineteenth century. Earlier periods in the history of Christian thought were capable of devising a more unified approach to theology. Farley and Pannenberg acknowledge, moreover, that the history of the concept of theology and its problems offers some hope for a solution to the present impasse. Farley finds the solution on the subjective and formational side of the problem, while Pannenberg locates it on the objective, scientific side.

Ebeling does not offer a specific solution to the problem. He does, however, indicate a direction. Ebeling looks toward a

---

[4]Cf., further, below, chap. 4.

[5]See below, appendix to chap. 1.

"fundamental theology" that is essentially hermeneutical or interpretive as the key to unity. Within the larger interpretive structure identified by this "fundamental theology," the various disparate disciplines would maintain their integrity and their distinct methodologies, but each would assume the interpretive task of identifying the truth toward which it points. Ebeling's fundamental theology, with its concentration on this question of truth, would draw the disciplines toward a union that lies beyond their individual competency but also arises out of the basic intention and direction of each discipline. Although there are major differences between Ebeling and Pannenberg, both point toward an objective unity of the various disciplines into a single theology or study of theology.

The proliferation of subdisciplines does not necessarily destroy the unity of such a paradigm, just as the proliferation of techniques necessary to the accomplishment of a large task does not destroy the possibility of a cohesive outcome. This diversity may simply mean that there has been an inward diversification of specializations under the larger fourfold curricular model. The model may need some explanation and interpretation, but it may still serve as a pattern for organizing the various subdisciplines. Indeed, it may offer a pattern for an overarching interpretive "fundamental theology."

In his discussion of the historicity and temporal relativity of theologies, Ebeling also introduces a major problem that does not seem to have troubled either Farley or Pannenberg. Theologies supercede one another historically and stand alongside one another in opposition and even mutual contradiction today. In striving for their own theological understanding of the unity of theology, both Farley and Pannenberg implicitly fall under Ebeling's warning: they address only a segment, never the whole of the theological community. The problems of historicity and relativity are not, however, in and of themselves, dangers or insurmountable barriers to theological understanding in the present. On the one hand, a superceded theology does not necessarily lose all relevance to the future simply by being superceded. A theological cul-de-sac like Arianism is superceded by Nicene orthodoxy largely because, considered as a perspective on God, Christ, and redemption, it does not work: it was not simply superceded in time, it was set aside with good reason. The post-Nicene theology of the Cappadocian fathers was, however, simply superceded—particularly in the Latin West. It was appropriated in the fourth century by writers like Victorinus, Hilary, and Ambrose and superceded in the fifth century by Augustine's grand Trinitarian vision. Nonetheless, the Cappadocian theology remains a useful resource, a point for critique of Trinitarianism in the present.[6]

On the other hand, mutually exclusive theologies are—or at least ought to be—capable of enlightening one another. I know, for example, that "Death of God" theology is and must be quite unacceptable to evangelical Christians. Evangelical theology rests on the certainty that the God of the Bible and the church cannot die and cannot cease to be of significance. Nonetheless, when we look at the incredible secularization of American culture and see how little place secular culture allows for the divine and also just how many churches and congregations participate in that secularization and by their fundamental accommodation to the culture effectively rule God out of large segments of human life, then the particular construction given to the phrase "Death of God" by Gabriel Vahanian becomes particularly significant. We may not like what we read in Vahanian's book—but we have to recognize the accuracy of the indictment even now, some twenty years later.

The diversity itself, then, inasmuch as it is neither a barrier to learning nor a hindrance to theological formulation, does not stand in the way of a unified theological understanding. It merely makes us aware that the diversity or pluralism of the modern world must somehow be dealt with in the search for unity. Another way to make this point is simply to recognize that a unity of perspective ought not to be gained by a sectarian procedure of narrowing the theological focus until our picture contains only those views that we find congenial.

Farley's critique pinpoints a general problem in the

---

[6]Cf. Robert Jenson, *The Triune Identity: God According to the Gospel* (Philadelphia: Fortress, 1982).

contemporary American perception of theology. Although the problem is not evidenced uniformly throughout the country, it is certainly true that American seminaries and churches have tended to externalize the unity of theology by emphasizing the practice of ministry and, further, by defining practice in terms of the techniques of ministry. Again, it is not a universal problem uniformly evidenced, but the teachers of ministerial practice have been notoriously unable to deal with theological issues drawn from biblical, historical, or dogmatic theology and to apply these issues to contemporary situations. (There is also considerable irony in the frequently heard claim that the teachers of the so-called theoretical disciplines ought to make their courses more practical when the teachers of practice have difficulty working with theological categories.) Farley is correct, too, when he notes that the denominational and clerical emphasis on technique has become, retroactively, a barrier to the merger of nominally theoretical and nominally practical concerns in theological education. All too often it seems that the theoretical subjects are necessary for obtaining the degree, but not necessary for carrying on subsequent ministry. The result is that both education and ministry suffer.

Even so, Farley points to a genuine need in theological education and in subsequent engagement in the theological tasks of ministry when he focuses on *paideia* defined, in a classical sense, as an understanding related to the cultivation of character and culture. Theological understanding, defined as an inward, interpretive theological disposition, must be a goal of theological training. I differ with Farley, however, on his location of the unity of theology primarily on the subjective side of the study in the cultivation of theological understanding.

The greatest problem that a more classical approach to theology will have with Farley's argument stems from his willingness to set aside the objective foundation of the older concept of *theologia*. He no longer views as possible the derivation of the unity of the discipline from the unity of its object. Instead, the unity of the discipline is to be defined functionally, inasmuch as the *theologia* that Farley recovers is "salvation viewed as a self-conscious interpretive activity."

From a classical perspective, the unity of interpretive activity must arise out of the unity of the discipline itself, not out of the singularity of the interpreter.

In his discussion of the shift of theology "from unitary discipline to aggregate of specialties," Farley argues that, prior to the Enlightenment, "the norms for theology" or *principia* of theology were the articles of faith, the "doctrines of church tradition." With the rise of critical methodologies in the Enlightenment and the application of critical historical, philological, and hermeneutical methods to Scripture, now viewed as a body of data, Scripture became the object of various diverse "sciences" or disciplines, and each theological activity, exegetical, historical, dogmatic, became a specialized science in its own right.[7] On the one hand, Farley is quite correct in recognizing the critical methods of the Enlightenment as bringing about a separation of disciplines. Most notable is the rise of biblical theology as a historical description of the religion of Israel or of the New Testament church. On the other hand, Farley is somewhat mistaken in his identification of *principia* and therefore in his view of the pre-Enlightenment unity of the discipline.

Although late medieval writers who spoke of foundations or *principia* did identify them as the articles of faith, the Protestant orthodox, both Lutheran and Reformed, adapted the term to the *sola Scriptura* of the Reformation and to a more philosophically adequate identification of *principia* with *archai*. The *archai*, the ultimate or truly foundational principles available to theology were God, the principle of being or essential foundation, and Scripture, the principle of knowing or cognitive foundation.[8] This view of the Protestant language gives us quite a different perception of the unity of theology in the pre-Enlightenment phase of Protestantism from that given by Farley's analysis. The methods, tools, and approaches used in theology could be quite diverse; theology could be practical and

---

[7]Farley, *Theologia*, pp. 40–42.

[8]See Richard A. Muller, *Post-Reformation Reformed Dogmatics*, vol. 1: *Prolegomena* (Grand Rapids: Baker, 1987), pp. 295–311.

theoretical in its emphases; and the ability to understand "divine things" could vary from subject to subject—but theological knowledge as such could still be regarded as a unity because of the singleness of its cognitive foundation, its *principium cognoscendi*. And resting on that unity, theology could further identify the unity of its subject matter, its "substance" or its "object" of study.

In other words, there is an unnecessary dichotomy underlying Farley's arguments. In contrasting the pre-Enlightenment with the post-Enlightenment view of theology he writes:

> Insofar as theology is a habitus of practical wisdom which attends salvation, it has no additional end since the existential, saving knowledge of God is itself the end for which the human being is created. In that way of thinking, theology itself is the end (telos) of the study of theology. On the other hand, when theology names an objective referent, doctrinal truths, and when it is a generic term for a faculty of disciplines, then it does need an end beyond itself, and the training of clergy is an obvious solution to that problem.[9]

In the first place, the older view of theology as "a habitus of practical wisdom" did not at all place the end of theology within theology itself. Rather, the identification of theology as practical was intended to indicate specifically that the discipline was oriented toward a goal beyond itself! This same theology also defined theology as theoretical or contemplative, indicating that theological knowledge was capable of being an end in itself. Indeed, the older theology debated at length the question of how theology could be theoretical or practical or a combination of *theoria* and *praxis*.[10] Theology is an objective knowledge, valuable in itself (theory) that has as its goal (praxis) the union of the believer with God, the highest good.

In the second place, the language of *theoria* and *prax.* typical of this older theology, whether medieval or orthodox

---

[9]Farley, *Theologia*, p. 82.
[10]Cf. Muller, *Post-Reformation Reformed Dogmatics*, chap. 6, section 3.

Protestant, did not in any way alter the fact that theology was understood both as an objective discipline composed of various subdisciplines and ancillary competencies and as a subjective disposition to know a certain body of knowledge. As a matter of fact, traditional theology assumed that a balance of objectivity and subjectivity needed to be maintained in the discussion of theology and the study of theology. The unity of the discipline of theology in the older Protestantism did not arise out of an absence of subdisciplines. Nor did it arise, as Ebeling's arguments seem to indicate, out of an absence of diverse methodologies. There were, after all, distinctions made in sixteenth- and seventeenth-century Protestantism between the study of Old and New Testament, the study of "positive" or didactic theology, the study of polemical theology, and the study of ancillary disciplines such as language, logic, and philosophy. In the seventeenth century, practical theology and Christian rhetoric or homiletics took shape as disciplines. Nonetheless, theology was recognized as a unity according to its substance or object—God and God's works. Farley does recognize that the older theology differentiated between what we now call separate disciplines in terms of the way a theologian's cognitive disposition was directed toward its object, but what he does not fully acknowledge is that the unity of theology was considered to be objective, not subjective, arising out of the unity of *principium* and of substance, not out of the theologian's or pastor's cognitive powers.[11]

The fact that we can trace the origins of the fourfold model through the seventeenth and eighteenth centuries and the fact that the nineteenth-century framers of the modern "theological encyclopedia" either misunderstood or, as is more likely, altered the underlying rationale for the encyclopedia do not in and of themselves discredit the model. As we have seen in Pannenberg's argument for an objective unity of the disciplines into a single science, a historical analysis of the theological reasons for the separate disciplines can in fact reinforce the structure of the encyclopedia and, in addition,

---

[11]Cf. Farley, *Theologia*, p. 40.

indicate its unity. Beyond this, Farley's assumption that neither the authority of Scripture nor salvation history are viable concepts does not carry weight in all parts of the theological world! In addition, because the canon of Scripture exists as a historically and theologically defined document distinct from the church-historical documents of the Christian community and functions in the church as no other document functions, it has its distinct theological function apart from, indeed, despite modern doubts concerning its authority, and even for those who express the doubts.

If Farley's rejection of "the way of authority," of a canon of Scripture, of a concept of salvation history, and of an identifiable divine revelation is unacceptable, there are nonetheless a series of insights in his study that are of major importance to us. He is entirely correct in identifying the central issue confronting theological study as the unification of that study around a *paideia*, a cultivation of theological understanding. He is also correct in seeing contemporary emphasis on ministerial technique as problematic. If technique governs theology, the whole enterprise is stood on its head and the actions that ought to be guided by a theological understanding of reality become the determinant of understanding. The result of this topsy-turvy approach to theology is stultifying.

The fourfold model, initially conceived with a view toward the organic unity of the disciplines, of itself does not necessarily result in a fragmentation of disciplines and a loss of the earlier unity of the theological disciplines. Whereas it is true, as Farley points out, that some of the nineteenth-century encyclopedists assumed that the four areas of the model were four neatly defined disciplinary areas, it is also true that several of the major encyclopedists, like Luthardt and Räbiger, recognized that the biblical, historical, systematic, and practical areas simply identify broad types or categories of study that relate to one another in the life of the church. Right use of the basic fourfold pattern ought not necessarily to exclude any disciplines useful to the church, nor should it cause "the question of faith and science" to be "isolated as a subquestion" dealt with occasionally in one or another of the various and sundry

subdisciplines.[12] Much of the burden of this book is to take
seriously Farley's critique of the fourfold model as it has often
been represented and used, but also to argue the usefulness of
the model when it is understood as an interpretive tool that
unifies the various biblical, historical, systematic, and practical
disciplines in and for the work of theological formulation, with
theology itself being understood as the "science of the Christian
religion."[13]

Much more telling is Farley's perception of the alteration
of the practical aspect of theology from a sense of goal-
directedness to a category training in ministerial practice. The
danger of the shift from a view of all theology as involved in a
praxis to a part of theology identified as practice lies in the
tendency of this separated—and internally fragmented—practice to cause us to lose sight of its theological underpinnings and
of its relation to the other subdisciplines in the curriculum,
particularly the so-called theoretical ones. "Theory," too, has
shifted in meaning—instead of indicating the character of
theology as worth knowing in and for itself, it has come to
indicate a nonpractical intellectual superstructure, somehow
bracketing and guiding the practice of ministry. Here, too, the
unity of theological study and the clear line of movement from
biblical interpretation to contemporary faith-statement and
ministry are obscured by the potential fragmentation of disciplines.

I am convinced that there is considerably less irony than
Farley notes in the conservative adoption of the fourfold
encyclopedia, inasmuch as certain nineteenth-century encyclopedists—notably Luthardt, Hagenbach, Schaff, and Kuyper—
were already moving toward the reconstruction or reevaluation
of the fourfold model in terms of their historical grasp of older
theological perspectives. In addition, and perhaps more importantly, the fourfold model, as developed in the wake of Gabler

---

[12]Ibid., p. 134.

[13]It is worth noting that Farley recognizes this nineteenth-century option
(ibid., p. 138) but has not worked out its transmission into the twentieth
century at the hands of Pannenberg.

and Schleiermacher, embodies the recognition, even among the more conservative theological educators, that a major change had taken place in the study of theology during the eighteenth and early nineteenth centuries and that even a more traditionalistic model than that proposed by Schleiermacher had to bear those changes in mind.

Of considerably greater impact on the study of theology than the nineteenth-century attempt to gather the various theological disciplines into a three- or fourfold encyclopedia was the rise of the historical-critical method and the development of new approaches in hermeneutics. What presently stands in the way of a unified approach to theological study, far more than the gathering of the disciplines into four groups, is the critical approach to the text of Scripture. Inasmuch as modern critical methods focus primarily on the meaning of the text in its ancient historical situation, they can create barriers to the closure of the "hermeneutical circle"—barriers to the attempt of hermeneutics to draw text and interpreter together and to bring the ancient meaning to bear, with contemporary significance, on the present situation.[14] These barriers continue to exist, at least in part, because the study of theology as a whole has not kept pace with the hermeneutical developments of the last several centuries. We cannot move from Scripture to systematic theology and ministry in the way the medieval doctors or the seventeenth-century Protestant orthodox did because the alteration of approach to the text of Scripture demands a wholly different approach not only to the other disciplines but also and more importantly to their interrelationship.

We have already observed, with Farley, the importance of an altered view of theory and praxis to the reconstruction of theological study. The resources for this aspect of the reconstruction come from the older, precritical theology. A second resource or set of resources come directly from the critical

---

[14]Some of the difficulties brought on by changes in hermeneutics, together with insights into the value of older exegetical methods, are presented in Silva, *Has the Church Misread the Bible?* chap. 4.

developments of the eighteenth and nineteenth centuries. In addition to the rise of practical theology, these centuries witnessed the rise of historical theology. The eighteenth century began with a group of writers—most notably Mosheim and Walch—who attempted to replace the chronologically arranged polemics of the older theology with an objective discussion of history. The result of their labors was the rise of the modern discipline of historical theology and, as a by-product in the hands of Semler and others, the historical–critical method together with its attendant hermeneutical insights. If critical, textual, and historical methods have caused some disruption of traditional theology, they have also brought a clearer sense of the meaning of Scripture while the historical discipline itself has provided theology with a far more accurate sense of its own roots and of its resources for formulation. Indeed, the consciousness of history provides an insight into the character of the entire theological task that, together with a recovery of the concepts of theory and praxis and with a use of modern hermeneutical insights, can lead to a unification of theological study.

It is also true that part of the problem of theological education is the separation of the university-based study of religion from the seminary-based study of theology. The university has retained a sense of the personally formative character of education while the seminary has retained materials of theology without a sense of their intrinsically formative character. Farley recognizes this curious impasse but, after rejecting traditional patterns of authority, does not offer a clear way past the problem. He does not provide a definition of the way in which the "truth" and the "reality" toward which the various materials of theology point can be identified and grasped. Although Farley would probably object to this criticism of his conclusions as tending to reduce "theological understanding" to a particular form of study, the proper solution to this problem of university-seminary split and of curricular disunity seems to be the development not only of an attitude toward study but also of a material unity of the curriculum resting on a legitimation of the theological disciplines as together constituting a unified science and possessing, in their unity, a single object of knowledge. This criticism points us clearly in the direction indicated both by pre-Enlightenment orthodoxy and, in our own time, by Pannenberg.

It is regrettable that the university model, with its drive toward uncommitted objectivity, retains an interest in *paideia* and the cultivation of understanding while the seminary-model with its sense of commitment has lost much of its interest in *paideia* and the cultivation of understanding. It is also unfortunate that there is a bifurcation of commitment and objectivity— particularly because these categories are not mutually exclusive. Again, Pannenberg provides a useful insight even if we do not adopt his model in all of its detail: theology can and ought to be constructed and studied with a view toward objectivity and toward the proper use of historical, critical, and hermeneutical tools. If the basic character of religion in general and of Christianity in particular is historical, the right use of critical and hermeneutical tools, grounded as they are in historical understanding, cannot ultimately be a problem. Commitment to the historical faith does not rule out, indeed, can be enhanced by, historical objectivity in method.

Over against the inherent subjectivism of Farley's approach we can place Pannenberg's insistence on the objective character of theology, even if the object of theological science can only be presented and analyzed indirectly as a problem to be solved or a hypothesis to be proved. Pannenberg's approach has not only an affinity for the more traditional view of theology (at least on this particular point), but it also has the virtue of presenting theology as a genuine academic discipline capable of maintaining its place among the disciplines. We must question only the second part of the proposal, that God is a problem to be solved or a hypothesis to be proven. This approach has merit in a purely academic context, but the churchly perspective of the seminary and the normative character of theology as studied and used in ministry demand something more—in short, both seminary and parish demand faith in the existence of God, as testified in Scripture and tradition, as the beginning point of study and of proclamation.

The seemingly insurmountable barrier standing in the way of an American attempt to realize Pannenberg's schema for a theological curriculum is the opposition, typical of American education, between the history-of-religions approach usually associated with college and university-based, secular study and the churchly, theological and ministerial approach associated with seminary-based study, whether liberal or conservative. Farley recognizes this problem but offers no real solution other than the inclusion of the study of non-Christian religions or of comparative religion in the seminary curriculum. He provides no model comparable to that of Pannenberg for discerning the objective or scientific unity of this study of religion with the rest of the curriculum. To find such a unity in and for the churchly purposes of the seminary would probably demand a return to and a successful completion of the quest, indicated by Ernst Troeltsch in the first quarter of this century, for a definition of the "absoluteness of Christianity" in the context of world religion.[15] Troeltsch's insight, long neglected in many parts of the theological world because of neoorthodoxy's myopic rejection of the concepts of religion as a merely human phenomenon and of natural revelation as universally accessible, has come of age in the global community of the late twentieth century. The question that Troeltsch raises, of course, is how to maintain the absoluteness or ultimacy of the Christian message once it is acknowledged for the sake of objectivity in study that Christianity is a religion among the religions. Neoorthodoxy ignored the question and claimed, without clear warrant, the absoluteness of Christianity.

The great danger here is that, because of the possible pitfalls of the approach, we ignore the mandate to study Christianity historically, as a historical religion in the context of

---

[15]Cf. Ernst Troeltsch, *The Absoluteness of Christianity and the History of Religion*, trans. David Reid (Richmond: John Knox, 1971), and note that Pannenberg's theological project points in this very direction; see his *Theology and the Philosophy of Science*, trans. Francis McDonagh (Philadelphia: Westminster, 1976), especially pp. 301–45, 358–71, and his essay "Toward a Theology of the History of Religions," in *Basic Questions in Theology*, trans. George Kehm, 2 vols. (Philadelphia: Westminster, 1983), 2:65–118.

world history. Each of the views of the study of theology has, in its own way, underlined the importance of the historical and of the investigation of Christianity as a religion in history. Without arguing for a fundamental unity of theologia out of which to construct a unified pattern of study and thought, Ebeling does emphasize the universal scope of church history as a bridge from biblical study and the general study of religion to the various ancillary disciplines (the humanities and the sciences, natural and social) and to the standard contemporizing disciplines—practical theology, dogmatics, ethics, and fundamental theology. Farley clearly sees the study of history—particularly the history of the concept of theology and of the organized study of theology—as the key to our present-day recovery of unified and meaningful theological study. For Pannenberg, the concept of history and the history of religion take on a fundamental theological significance.

Each of these perceptions can be carried over into our approach to the study of theology. Church history and the history of doctrine do establish a broad perspective for the study of Christianity and do have the effect of bridging the gap between biblical study and the various contemporizing disciplines. They do this both by providing a historical link connecting the past of the religious community with its present and by revealing the way in which the church has developed disciplines like dogmatics, ethics, and practical theology in the past and has folded materials from literature, philosophy, and the sciences into its teaching. Knowledge of this historical path provides both positive and negative models for the present—the recovery of useful concepts and tools from the past, the identification of the origins and reasons for ongoing problems, and the clarification not only of the ideas and teachings we presently hold but also of ways in which useful and valid ideas and teachings are constructed within the community of faith and brought to bear on its present. Finally, the historical and religious trajectory of Christianity has its own theological significance when it is understood as the fundamental reality of the life of the community of faith and as the key to our own grasp of the ongoing significance of the biblical and churchly materials that remain, today, the primary statements of the faith of Christians.

How, then, can a unified approach to theological study be constructed? If my presentation and critique of Ebeling, Farley, and Pannenberg *are* correct, a unified approach to the study of theology must begin with a clear understanding of the sources of theology and their mutual interrelation. This interrelation must be understood, moreover, both historically and, with a view toward the fundamental historical reality of the faith, with a methodological and interpretive consistency. Method and interpretation must, in turn, reflect the needs of theology as a discipline or "science" that stands objectively on its foundations and materials and also functions subjectively in the context of human understanding. The human understanding cultivated in theology must involve a construction and analysis of reality, of God, the world, and our place before God in the world. This consideration points, finally, to a balance in theology of theory and praxis, of knowledge known in and for itself and of knowledge known for the sake of attaining a goal—that mirrors the balance of the objective and subjective aspects of the study.

This balance of the subjective and the objective, of the theoretical and the practical depends on the clear identification of Christianity, not only in our definition of its reality but also in our approach to the study of theology, as both a religion with its own history and a revelation given and understood historically in a particular religion. The historical character of the religion and its revelation provides a basis in Christianity itself for the positive use of contemporary hermeneutics. Indeed, it yields a promise that the historical approach to Scripture dictated by modern hermeneutics will have a positive result in the construction of a model for the study of the whole of Christianity and for the formulation of contemporary definitions of Christian faith, whether in theological system or in the contextualization of the church's message in preaching and witness. The religious character of Christianity, moreover, provides a basis in Christianity itself for the positive relationship of theory and practice. It holds a promise that the ongoing life and worship of the community—its religion and spirituality—point both toward the possibility of an objectively grounded statement of the meaning of Christianity on a theoretical level and toward the possibility of a well-defined practice directly related to and drawing guidance from the theoretical statement.

APPENDIX:
CONTEMPORARY PROBLEMS AND INSIGHTS: THREE APPROACHES

Ebeling's *Study of Theology*

Gerhard Ebeling's eminent introduction to theological study begins with the statement "The study of theology is beset by a crisis in orientation."[16] Ebeling speaks of a disruption of "access to the unity and totality that constitutes the subject matter of theology"; and the fact that, in the absence of this unity, "the domain of the subject matter and tasks" of theology has not only diversified but "broken apart and crumbled" into isolated disciplines and subdisciplines. In addition, Ebeling argues that this absence of "inner unity" is reflected by the erosion of the relationship between theology and the "totality of the experience of reality."[17] These problems are not entirely new—they have identifiable historical roots—but they have been intensified in the twentieth century.

The study of theology, Ebeling continues, is fraught with tensions. Theology is an ecclesial discipline that experiences a built-in tension between scholarship and vocation. On the one hand, the necessity of being a generalist concerned with the life of congregations and churches can become a barrier to ongoing meditation on theological problems, and "academic study appears to be more of a hindrance than a preparation"; once a student has received the basic theological degree, there is little incentive to continue studying the materials of theology. On the

---

[16]Gerhard Ebeling, *The Study of Theology*, trans. Duane Priebe (Philadelphia: Fortress, 1978), p. 1.

[17]Ibid.

other hand, study can become an island unto itself, detached from vocation. The reason that these two opposite tendencies represent a tension and not simply a congenial separation of interests and specializations is that "what is called the study of theology in the technical sense is only the introduction to the continuous study of theology in a person's vocation."[18] At least this is the purpose of technical study and the ideal tendency of vocation!

Theology, no matter how scholarly its exercise, always "involves something that does not seem compatible with scholarship": it deals with revelation of and faith in God, neither of which can be subservient to the techniques and methods of scholarship. When theology has a "scholarly character," therefore, it has that character only in the context of vocation and faith. Theology, according to Ebeling, cannot be justified as a discipline among other disciplines, as a "science" among other "sciences," according to generalized scholarly criteria. Without denying the need and the place for theological scholarship, it must also be recognized that the scholarship itself is finally responsible to the faith and that faith, the life, the vocation, is not lessened in importance because it fails to maintain contact with a mass of scholarly literature.

In addition to this basic tension between study and vocation, Ebeling notes three basic problems that arise out of "the historicity of theology": first, theologies "supercede one another historically"; second, theologies can and do "substantively exclude each other"; and third, within theology "there are disciplines that compete methodologically."[19] In each case, the historical diversity of theologies stands in the way of a unity of approach in theology. The first of these problems can be defined by the fact that "theologies cannot be conserved or repristinated." Theology does not move from lesser to greater or from worse to better—frequently the reverse seems to be closer to the truth, but the old cannot be retained inasmuch as theology must be rooted in its historical context and therefore

---

[18]Ibid., p. 3.
[19]Ibid., pp. 5–8.

must move forward in time, although not necessarily toward a higher or better form of expression. If a unity can be detected in this succession of theologies, that unity must arise out of the subject matter of theology as it is reflected under different conditions and in different circumstances.

The second problem is equally serious: theologies do not merely succeed one another, they also frequently stand alongside one another in opposition and contradiction. Not only are there the traditional opposition of heresy and orthodoxy and of one confessional "orthodoxy" to another, there are also the theologies, typical of the present age, that do not fit precisely into any of these traditional categories. Confessional theologies no longer seem to be "definitive," Ebeling notes, and "the decisive theological fronts appear to cut across them."[20] The unity of theology, identified by the subject matter, is not a unity that carries over into the articulation of that subject matter. Theological agreement is difficult to achieve in our century— and any unity that we find must be able to deal with multiplicity of forms and diversity of statements.

Whereas the first and second problems tend to stand in the way of any single analysis of the study of theology becoming normative throughout the Christian community, the third problem noted by Ebeling stands in the way of any unified analysis of the study of theology, even one that is limited in its address to a particular and fairly homogeneous segment of the larger Christian community. There are a host of theological disciplines and subdisciplines that, in Ebeling's words, "compete methodologically." By this Ebeling means that the organization and unity of the disciplines is not achieved as a simple movement from the biblical materials through the history of the church and its doctrines into our own time in systematic and practical theology. Although the materials certainly line up chronologically in this way, the question of the methodology to be followed in contemporary system and practice forces us to recognize that the issue is complex. Tracing out the history of a problem does not automatically provide a

---

[20]Ibid., p. 6.

solution in the present: Is dogmatic theology to follow an exegetical or a "systematic" method? How does biblical theology relate to dogmatics now that it is an independent discipline rather than a part of the dogmatic enterprise? There are, as Ebeling notes, "competing claims" of the historical and the systematizing disciplines.[21]

Ebeling's recognition of this host of problems leads him to conclude that there is an unresolvable tension underlying theological study in the present day and that his own essay on the study of theology can only be a "reflection about the individual disciplines," each in its own methodological integrity. He is unable to develop a "systematic deduction of the disciplines from the nature of theology" or to present a unitive schema that includes all of the theological disciplines. Nonetheless Ebeling does wish to draw out connections and relationships in the hope that a clearer view of the "whole of theology" will emerge from his discussion. He thus begins with the New Testament as foundational to Christianity; proceeds via the Old Testament and the study of religion and philosophy to the "most universal theological discipline," church history; and from that universal basis looks out on the ancillary disciplines in order, finally, to draw the whole together in practical theology, dogmatics, ethics, and "fundamental" or interpretive, hermeneutical theology. When he has done so, then at last the question of unity can again be raised at the level of the foundational truth embodied in the subject-matter of the several disciplines.[22]

Ebeling's work raises a series of issues that cannot be ignored. They must be settled or in some way set aside if the study of theology is ever to be conceived or undertaken as a unified whole. In the first place, the problem of tension between scholarship and vocation can hardly be done away with, inasmuch as the sacrifice of either side of the problem spells death to the whole theological enterprise. This problem will have to be incorporated into study as a basic fact of theological

---

[21]Ibid., pp. 7–8.
[22]Ibid., pp. 8–11; cf. 156–58.

existence. In the second place, some decision will have to be made concerning the relationship of the disciplines and subdisciplines of theology to one another, and this decision will have to involve historical and methodological choices. Such choices will create as well as solve problems: to the extent that Ebeling feels he cannot make those choices and must sacrifice the larger unity of the discipline, he fails to solve the basic problem that he poses—but to the extent that we move beyond the impasse noted by Ebeling, we will also exclude options that his approach left open.

Farley's *Theologia*

One of the more important attempts to come to terms on a theoretical level with the study of theology and its problems is Edward Farley's *Theologia: The Fragmentation and Unity of Theological Education* (1983). Farley's work is important because its arguments rest on an extensive evaluation of the history of the study of theology and because it addresses, quite specifically, the American scene. Farley begins his argument with a historical overview of the study of theology in which he points out that theology, as studied in the Middle Ages and in the Reformation and post-Reformation eras, was regarded as a knowledge (*scientia*) or a wisdom (*sapientia*) directed toward salvation. This view of theology was not only cognitive, it was also grounded on doctrinal governing-principles and controlled methodologically as a unified academic discipline in its own right. With the rise of pietism and the dawn of the Enlightenment, this view of theology was challenged and, Farley argues, brought to an end. The unity of theological education has been lost and this loss is "responsible more than anything else for the problematic character of that education as a course of study."[23] Unlike Ebeling, however, Farley hopes to find a unified approach to the study of theology.

In order to isolate the problem and pose a solution, Farley presses quickly beyond the older patterns of the Middle Ages,

---

[23]Farley, *Theologia*, p. ix.

the Reformation, and the post-Reformation era and concentrates the historical portion of his study on the development of "theological encyclopedia" during the Enlightenment and in the nineteenth century. Before the Enlightenment, the various disciplines and subdisciplines of theology were studied reverently for the purpose of "forming" in the mind "that sapiential knowledge called theologia." This knowledge was, in turn, the proper foundation for the exercise of ministry. The Enlightenment marks a major change in attitude toward both the disciplines and the rationale for studying them. Farley points to Mosheim and Semler as inaugurators of this change: for Mosheim, theological study is not the cultivation of a disposition to know a particular unified wisdom or knowledge so much as training in a set of disciplines useful to leaders in the church; for Semler, similarly, theological study is training in skills for the sake of cultivating the "dexterity proper to teachers of the Christian religion." In other words, study is no longer unified by a sense of a single object of knowing but by a sense of the practical application of the diverse theological disciplines.[24]

Similarly, the rationalism of the eighteenth century conjoined to historical method wreaked havoc on traditional theology. Farley goes so far as to call this alliance a "hermeneutics of destruction" that led to the identification of "discrete efforts of inquiry and scholarship, each applying rational and historical principles." The theology that had once been drawn together as a unity and maintained in a unified form by Protestants in particular under the theme of an authoritative Scripture, was no longer an academic possibility.[25]

The development of "theological encyclopedia," beginning around 1760 and extending through the nineteenth century, takes for granted these basic shifts in emphasis and definition accomplished in the first half of the eighteenth century. The various so-called theological encyclopedias all attempt to define the disciplines that belong to the study of

---

[24]Ibid., pp. 62–63.
[25]Ibid., p. 65.

theology and to identify the pattern and unity of those disciplines. By the end of the eighteenth century there had emerged the basic fourfold pattern of three "theoretical" disciplines (biblical, historical, and systematic) and the practical field. This fourfold pattern marks the emergence of church history from polemical theology as a positive discipline aiding in the formulation of doctrine and in the present-day formation of personal piety. It also marks the redefinition of "practical" theology as the application of the truths of the theoretical disciplines by the clergy in preaching, catechesis, and the care of souls.[26]

The disciplines gathered together in the theological encyclopedias do reflect the categories of theological literature set forth in guide-books of the orthodox era, but virtually none of these essays in encyclopedia reflects an orthodox understanding of theology as "divinely imparted knowledge" resting on God's archetypal self-knowledge. Scripture is retained as the foundation of theologizing, but Scripture itself is now viewed historically and critically. As Farley points out, the encyclopedia itself, for all its "orthodox" appearance, is a postorthodox phenomenon, reflecting a postorthodox conceptuality. The encyclopedia itself is rooted in the separation of disciplines and subdisciplines—of history from polemical theology, of practical theology from the application of biblical and systematic study, of biblical theology both from exegesis strictly defined and from dogmatic or systematic theology. The disciplines as we understand them today were defined for us by the nineteenth century in the wake of Schleiermacher.[27]

These historical considerations point toward a problem inherent in the encyclopedia itself. On the one hand, the unified study of theology as a theoretical-practical, biblical-historical discipline was possible in the context of "the confessional churches of Protestantism." In theological terms, Farley argues, "the great Reformed and Lutheran dogmatic structures functioning within the Protestant 'way of authority' is the founda-

---

[26]Ibid., pp. 78–80.
[27]Ibid. p. 81.

tion of the initial Protestant encyclopedia." Since theology was considered, in these dogmatic systems, as "a single thing, the knowledge of God and divine things as it is given in the written form of revelation, the inspired Scriptures," the study of theology could also be "one thing."[28] On the other hand, the postorthodox, Enlightenment construction of the fourfold encyclopedia meant that the various disciplines came to be viewed as methodologically independent areas of study. Theology, as defined in this fourfold curriculum, was "no longer one thing but an umbrella term for a number of different enterprises." Their unity was derived not from a cognitive, objective unity of *theologia* but from a "clerical paradigm" focused on the minister and the competencies needs "for ministry."[29] The victory of the "clerical paradigm" has meant the loss of an internal, intellectual, and spiritual motive and goal for theology. The loss of this sense of a single unified theological wisdom, Farley quite convincingly argues, has resulted in the dispersion of the encyclopedia into a series of unrelated specializations— subdisciplines that do not interrelate and do not cooperate to produce a single knowledge called theology. The subdisciplines have distinguished themselves independently as academic exercises but they no longer function together to produce a *paideia*, a unified teaching that can be directed toward the goal of ministry.

The American scene is, as Farley's essay recognizes, quite different from the European. The tension seen by Ebeling between scholarship and vocation appears, in the American context, as a total separation of concerns. In the same vein Farley writes, "The present ethos of the Protestant churches is such that a theologically oriented approach to the preparation of ministers is not only irrelevant but counterproductive." Theology is studied in seminary but not practiced in the parish. "At its very best, a theological education is only the beginning of career-long discipline, and it is just this continuing 'study of

---

[28]Edward Farley, "The Reform of Theological Education," in *Theological Education* 17,2 (Spring 1981): 96.

[29]Ibid., p. 98.

theology' which does not occur."[30] The point is stated radically, but it is substantially correct. It is also, as Farley argues, ironic inasmuch as the study of theology, for most of the history of the church, did in fact nourish ministry.

When theology is reduced to "a pedagogy for ministerial education," it may be justified by "practice," but at the same time, Farley recognizes, "practice in its widest and most significant sense is systematically eliminated from the structure of theological study." When theology was defined as a mental or spiritual disposition, practice was an integral part of theology as a whole inasmuch as all theological study, whether nominally biblical or historical or dogmatic, was directed toward personal formation. When theological study is restrictively directed toward the techniques of ministry, practice is made "external to theology" and the three "theoretical" areas of the encyclopedia are set over against the ministerial field. Part of the problem, Farley notes, is seen in the "exclusion of 'theology' from the university"—so that "theology," although taught as an academic specialty, is attached to the clerical paradigm and forced out of the broader realm of education. Theology functions neither in relation to the ministerial skills that dominate the seminary nor in relation to the larger issues of religious understanding assumed by the university to belong to the common property of human beings—i.e., to the laity![31]

Farley proposes a total reevaluation of the theological curriculum focused on the "recovery" of "*theologia* or theological understanding."[32] If *theologia* is to be recovered for theological education, there must be a revision not simply of the various subject-areas of theology in and for themselves but a new understanding of the entire theological enterprise. "Theological understanding" is not a subject-matter for study; as an example, Farley notes a course on the origins of Christianity in the first and second centuries. The issue is to teach this subject-matter in such a way that it contributes to theological understanding.

---

[30]Farley, *Theologia*, p. 4.
[31]Cf. ibid., pp. 133–34.
[32]Ibid., p. 151.

"Theology" is a matter of personal formation. In order to achieve this recovery of theology, moreover, the "clerical paradigm" must be discarded: training cannot focus on "the exercise of clerical activities," but rather it must emphasize a "general paideia" or "culturing" of human beings, a "shaping of human beings "under an ideal."[33]

This reform of theological education, Farley recognizes, cannot be accomplished purely at the graduate level: the interpretive skills necessary to study the materials of the church and its history, to understand the "origin, history, tradition, mythos and contemporary form" of the ecclesial representation of truth and reality, can only be learned over a lengthy "process of education."[34] "The life of encyclopedia is a dialectic of interpretation impelled by faith and its mythos occurring in and toward life's settings."[35] What Farley proposes, therefore, is not a curriculum but an approach to study. If something resembling the fourfold pattern is retained, it will be altered attitudinally and find its unity somewhere other than in ministerial practice—if a freer, more open-ended curriculum is adopted, the assumption is the same: its unity will be attitudinal and interpretive rather than based on an externalized goal of technique.

Pannenberg's *Theology and the Philosophy of Science*

The major study, in our time, of theology as a discipline is surely Wolfhart Pannenberg's *Theology and the Philosophy of Science*. The concern underlying Pannenberg's study is very different from that underlying Farley's. Although both writers perceive a threat to the integrity and unity of theology, Farley's analysis is geared to an intellectual community in which a deep split has long been recognized and, in some quarters, cherished, between the "academic study of religion" in the university and the ministerial or churchly study of theology in the seminary,

---

[33]Ibid., pp. 152–53, 179–81.
[34]Ibid., p. 183.
[35]Ibid., p. 185.

whereas Pannenberg's analysis is addressed to an intellectual community long accustomed both to church involvement in the university and to the acceptance of theology as a discipline alongside the other academic disciplines in the university curriculum. Farley's work, at least in part because of this divided mind of American religious studies, stresses the problem of viewing the study of theology as a "science." Pannenberg's, however, is directed precisely toward that end: the correct understanding of Christian theology as a "science" in the context of the other academic disciplines.

What is significant from the outset of Pannenberg's essay is his assumption that theology need not sacrifice either its traditional, churchly rootage and function or its academic, scientific integrity. He argues that theology "can be adequately understood only as a science of God." He disputes the view that theology must rest its integrity on either "a unity of method" or "the unity of a connection with practical activity" that is "external to its objects."[36] This concept of a unity resting on "practical activity" was the fruit of Schleiermacher's labors and an ultimate source of difficulty for theology—on the one hand, it could (and did) reduce theology to a historical and antiquarian discipline, while on the other it could (and did) generate a "positivistic" view of theology that placed theology outside the bounds of science and grounded it in a priori decision.[37]

In Pannenberg's view, we cannot escape the meaning of the term *theology* as determined by its history and embedded by that history in the discipline itself. Nor would it be desirable to escape: "God is the true object of theology," and theology is the study of the "divine economy" of "saving history, from creation to the eschatological fulfillment." Theology, then, recognizes God as its object and studies all things in their relation to God. Granting the reality of this relation, theology surmounts the problem of subjectivity and enters the realm of objective discipline, of science.[38] In the contemporary situation,

---

[36] *Theology and the Philosophy of Science*, p. 297.

[37] Ibid., pp. 297–98.

[38] Ibid., p. 298.

however, "God" is "under suspicion of being no more than a concept of faith." In other words, theology stands in danger of being reduced to a fideistic positivism, of losing its object. In order to find a solution to this problem and to retain the scientific objectivity necessary to a rightly conceived theology, Pannenberg proposes that theologians recognize the "openness . . . of the question of God" and approach God as the fundamental problem of the science of theology rather than as a dogma.[39]

This proposal, of course, raises another problem, inasmuch as it may reduce God to the status of a hypothesis and collapse theology into other disciplines, like "philosophical anthropology, psychology or sociology." Pannenberg sums up the issue:

> It is part of the finite nature of theological knowledge that even in theology the idea of God remains hypothetical and gives way to man's knowledge of the world and himself, by which it must be substantiated. On the other hand, as the theme of theology, God by definition includes the empirical reality by which the idea of God must be tested, and so defines the object of theology.[40]

The problem is, in a sense, circular. "The way in which God is to be understood as the object of theology therefore corresponds exactly to the problematic position of the idea of God in our experience."[41] God is known, Pannenberg argues, as a reality "co-given to experience in other objects" and known as the "all-determining reality" only by anticipation and hypothesis.

> The reality of God is always present only in subjective anticipations of the totality of reality in models of the totality of meaning presupposed in all particular experience. These models, however, are historic, which means that they are subject to confirmation or refutation by subsequent experience.[42]

---

[39]Ibid., p. 299.
[40]Ibid., p. 300.
[41]Ibid.
[42]Ibid.

Since reality as we know and experience it is not a finished whole but is part of a cosmic process, this view of religion as anticipatory places it into the realm of science. Granting, moreover, the connection between religion and theology, theology is, in fact, the science of religion. Pannenberg denies that theology is the science of religion in general—rather, he says, it is the science of "historic religions." Christian theology must, therefore, be defined as the "study of the Christian religion, the science of Christianity . . . in so far as it is the science of God."[43] Theology, as a science, examines historical religion with a view to determining how adequately religion deals with the experience of reality and, as a consequence, how adequately it identifies God as "the all-determining reality." "The traditional claims of a religion may therefore be regarded as hypotheses to be tested by the full range of currently accessible experience."[44] The further implication of this argument—which Pannenberg fully accepts—is that Christian theology must be regarded as a "specialized branch of theology in general," justified by the historical limits of Christianity and not by the personal faith of the theologian.[45]

This view of theological science leads Pannenberg directly to a descriptive statement of the organization of theological study. As a preparation for his presentation of the actual disciplines in the "theological encyclopedia," Pannenberg discusses "the relationship of the systematic and historical tasks in theology" and the "science of religion as theology of religion."[46] Theology is the science of God or the science that takes God as its object—but it approaches that object of "subject-matter only indirectly, through the study of religions."[47] This indirect approach is necessitated by the nature of theological knowing and points directly toward the historical as well as systematic approach characteristic of the study of theology.

[43]Ibid., pp. 314–15.
[44]Ibid., p. 315.
[45]Ibid., pp. 321–22.
[46]Ibid., pp. 346–71.
[47]Ibid., p. 346.

Theology is necessarily historical since it is a reflection on historical religion and specifically on historically located interpretations of God and world. Nonetheless, "theology cannot be just historical, because it is concerned not just with religious experiences, convictions and institutions of former ages, but also with deciding about their truth, deciding, that is to say, about the reality of God."[48]

The systematic side of theology arises precisely because the historical tradition of the religion mediates a religious meaning, a theological content, that must be investigated and assessed for the truth that is reflected in it. Historical knowledge, therefore, is the basis of systematic or constructive theology in the present. Pannenberg insists on this basic polarity of theology—materials that are necessarily addressed historically, particularly in view of the historical datum, the life and work of Christ, that lies at the heart of Christianity, but are also necessarily addressed systematically for the sake of a present-day statement of the content of faith and present-day assessment of its truth-claims. The various specialized fields of investigation—Old Testament and New Testament, church history, philology, and so forth—are an integral part of the theological task of discerning "the extent to which the particular historical data under investigation represents a self-communication of the all-determining divine reality."[49]

Pannenberg notes that any discussion of this theological task will manifest the difficulty of dividing the task into separate disciplines: the specializations are, of course, distinguishable, but this distinction is merely "pragmatic," inasmuch as the examination of the history of the religion for the sake of present-day systematization requires the concerted and cooperative effort of all disciplinary areas. One cannot systematize theology directly on the basis of reading the text of Scripture; such "theological exegesis," particularly as practiced by dialectical theology on the assumption of a "direct application" of biblical sayings to the present, lacks the requisite "historical

---

[48]Ibid., p. 347.
[49]Ibid., p. 348.

accuracy."[50] Nonetheless, theological interpretation, with reference to the present course of intellectual history and to
contemporary philosophical problems, is necessary to the task
of moving from the historical text to contemporary systematic
presentation. In reality, therefore, the task is a single, united
effort that transcends its division into disciplines and subdisciplines.

When the organization of theology into various disciplines
and subdisciplines is examined, Pannenberg quickly adds, this
organization is clearly more than merely pragmatic. The
creation of each independent discipline, when understood
historically, was a matter of theological and theoretical evaluation. Pannenberg insists that these historical and theological
grounds must be understood and the unity as well as the
distinction of the disciplines constructed for the present on the
basis of a clear historical understanding. It is self-defeating to
assume the validity of the present structure of theology and to
justify it after the fact, as was frequently done in the theological
encyclopedias of the last century.[51]

A primary distinction between biblical interpretation and
systematic theology can be discerned in the Middle Ages, but it
did not solidify into separate disciplinary areas until the
eighteenth century. The other disciplinary distinctions are more
recent.[52] It was the Protestant "rehabilitation" of scholastic
theology alongside biblical exegesis that created the disciplinary
distinction between the biblical and systematic fields for
Protestantism. In the eighteenth century this distinction, understood both in the light of pietist and rationalist or historicist
critique, became a distinction between biblical theology conceived as a historical investigation and dogmatic theology
understood as a present-day formulation resting on the historical materials.[53] Church history was separately studied for the
first time at the end of the sixteenth century and became a

---

[50]Ibid., pp. 348–49.
[51]Cf. ibid., p. 350.
[52]Ibid., p. 351.
[53]Ibid., pp. 355–56.

standardized area of study in the seventeenth, understood as part of the preparation for both polemical and dogmatic theology. Although lectures on pastoral theology were given from the Reformation onward, the separate discipline of practical theology arose only at the end of the eighteenth century, with its chief justification being provided in the nineteenth by Schleiermacher.[54]

The last discipline to be identified and given distinct academic status is the "science of religion"—which Pannenberg characterizes also as the "theology of religion." This discipline arose only at the very end of the nineteenth century and then only in profound debate. Many theologians, including Harnack, were so convinced of the "absoluteness" of Christianity that they took the study of Christianity as paradigmatic for the study of religion. The independence of the "science of religion" from dogmatic Christianity is recognized today, Pannenberg notes, in England, America, and Scandinavia—but not in Germany, at least not to the extent that Pannenberg believes is necessary. Christian theology, Pannenberg argues, can be correctly understood only "within the framework of a history of world religions."[55] Against the opposing view (which has all of the characteristics of neoorthodoxy) he remarks, "Only a dogmatic view of Christianity, which separates faith as knowledge of revelation from the world of religions, could treat religions as a phenomenon so external to Christianity as not to require consideration until missionary work makes Christianity look outwards."[56] In direct contradiction to this positivistic approach, Pannenberg declares that the spectrum of theological disciplines and subdisciplines can be rightly understood only in the context of the "science of religion."

This argument for a "science of religion" understood as a "theology of religion" provides the key to Pannenberg's vision of a unified study of theology that maintains for the most part the typical divisions of the discipline that have arisen during its

----

[54]Ibid., pp. 356–57.
[55]Ibid., p. 361.
[56]Ibid., pp. 361–62.

history. Indeed, inasmuch as the science of religion is an essentially historical investigation and inasmuch as history is the vehicle or means by which we receive and understand divine reality, the historical forms of that understanding have a lasting value and are not easily set aside; instead, they ought to be modified for use in the present. In this model, the foundational exercise would be the anthropologically grounded construction of a philosophy of religion in which the concept of religion could be defined "in connection with the objects of human experience of meaning, that is, so as to take account of the totality of meaning implicit in all experience of meaning, a totality which implies the existence of an all determining reality as its unifying unity."[57] This concept of religion in general would in turn lead to the development of a rightly constructed history of religions within which, in turn, "the religion of Israel and Christianity" could be correctly understood. Finally, within that understanding of Christianity, the various theological disciplines could be meaningfully presented.[58]

When he passes on to examine the particular disciplines belonging to Christian theology, Pannenberg draws together the subjects of biblical exegesis and church history as essentially historical in character. Nonetheless, the study of the history of theology must recognize the differences between biblical and church-historical study that led to their distinction as separate disciplines and must raise the question of the status of church history. Is church history a purely ancillary discipline as the Protestant orthodox of the seventeenth century and the neoorthodox of the twentieth, particularly Karl Barth, have argued?[59] Pannenberg resolves the question, at least tentatively, into one of canon: the distinction of biblical and churchly history rests on a dogmatic identification of the canon—the grouping of both disciplines into "historical theology" runs the risk of relegating the canon to a place of "secondary importance."[60]

---

[57]Ibid., p. 368.
[58]Ibid., p. 369.
[59]Ibid., p. 372.
[60]Ibid., p. 375.

While retaining the distinctive realms of the specialists, Pannenberg finds his overarching solution to this question in the history-of-religions model: "The history of religion in Israel, Judaism and primitive Christianity must be treated as a single process of tradition in which the spread of Christianity into the world of hellenism appears as only the last phase of a chain of receptions of non-Israelite religious traditions with Israel's religious consciousness."[61] The documents that are identified as canonical arose out of this history—and the goal of analyzing this literature in its proper literary, cultural, and historical context is the presentation of the religious tradition and its transmission from the era of ancient Israel to the period of primitive Christianity.

This study of the religious tradition of Israel and earliest Christianity is linked to the study of church history not only by the historical character of the investigation and the continuity of the history of earliest Christianity with the history of the church but also by the fact that church history is a discipline that "embraces the whole of theology."[62] Biblical exegesis is required, as a discipline, to restrict itself to the historical-critical task, whereas church history reaches out into biblical studies in its search for origins and presses forward, systematically and practically, in the present in its quest for explanation. It was the great mistake of Barthian theology to lower the status of history by severing church history from the apostolic age and by suppressing the historical questions raised by post-Reformation theology "in an attempt to make direct contact with the Reformation." As this mistake has become more and more obvious to theologians, church history has appeared more and more in the unifying discipline that connects the present of the church to its origins. The proper study of history will both clarify the problems of the present and manifest as yet untapped resources for theological formulation.[63]

Pannenberg can now point out that there is good reason to

---

[61]Ibid., p. 387.
[62]Ibid., p. 392.
[63]Ibid., pp. 392, 393.

describe dogmatics also as historical theology. Inasmuch as dogmatic or systematic theology is "the present formulation of the Christian doctrinal tradition," it is an essentially historical enterprise that must pass to a large extent under the critical judgment of church history. It is also the case that only the modes of presentation differ; the substance of systematic and historical theology is virtually identical. Granting, then, the rise of historical consciousness that made church history into an independent discipline, is there any reason to separate systematic theology from history as a discipline in its own right?[64] Pannenberg finds the identification of systematic theology as an organized study of the truths of Christianity in which their mutual interrelation is set forth and explained as fruitful in this regard: systematic theology can never be a field independent from historical theology, much less from historically adequate biblical exegesis, but its separate existence is justified precisely by its systematic character. Polemics and apologetics appear as natural subdivisions of the systematic task.

Christian ethics, which was historically considered a branch of the systematic exercise and did not become separated until the eighteenth and nineteenth centuries, can be viewed as the link connecting systematic with "practical" theology insofar as practical theology can be defined in "the ethics of action in the church."[65] Although practical theology has been typically defined as a separate discipline on the moral or ethical side of the curriculum, it is clearly also indicative of "the character of theology as a whole."[66] As a solution to the problems raised by attempts to ground practical theology in either dogmatics or ethics—or to view it as an instruction in church management— Pannenberg suggests "making the history of Christianity and the church the common basis of dogmatics, ethics, and practical theology" not in the sense of making it an antiquarian discipline, but in the sense as already indicated in his discussion of dogmatics, of viewing present practice as arising out of the

[64]Ibid., pp. 392, 405.
[65]Ibid., p. 423.
[66]Ibid., p. 424.

richness of the ongoing tradition of the church in the encounter with the present.[67]

From these three theologians we receive both a sense of the difficulty of the task that confronts the study of theology in the present and of the vast resources available to the church in the accomplishment of that task. Clearly, the study of theology in our time cannot simply be conducted according to older patterns of understanding. We are confronted by a differentiation and specialization of fields of study such that our theology cannot well serve the church unless a unifying perspective is also provided. Whereas Ebeling only hints at a hermeneutical or interpretive unity, Farley and Pannenberg point to this unity directly, with Pannenberg offering the more objective solution to the problem. The proposal offered in the present volume attempts to deal constructively with these three paradigms of study and to offer an approach to theology that does justice both to the need for an objective, historically and "scientifically" organized study of theology and to the equally important need for the recognition of the subjective aspect, both personal and corporate, of theological formulation in the present.

---

[67]Ibid., p. 435.

2

THE THEOLOGICAL
DISCIPLINES:
BIBLICAL AND HISTORICAL
FOUNDATIONS

It should be clear by now that the standard division of theological studies into the biblical, historical, systematic, and practical fields cannot rest either on the purely academic separation of four basic specializations or on the frequently made distinctions between theoretical and practical fields, classical and ministerial studies, or academic and spiritual or formational disciplines. The purely academic separation is a false separation inasmuch as all four fields are intimately related and, particularly in the cases of the systematic and practical fields, consistently use materials that belong to one or another of their collateral disciplines. The distinction between theoretical and practical is impossible to maintain because, on the one hand, it misunderstands the meanings in and for theology of *theoria* and *praxis* and, on the other, whatever definitions of these terms is accepted, the so-called theoretical disciplines are eminently practical while the practical disciplines are taught in the light of theoretical considerations. In the same way, the classical and academic disciplines belong to the life of ministry and spiritual formation while ministry and spiritual formation have been taken up into the disciplines of the academy.

Rather, as Pannenberg's arguments tend to confirm, the fourfold division of theological disciplines stands on a clear historical and functional basis that both makes necessary their distinction and, at the same time, renders impossible their

61

separation. The paradigm that is offered in this chapter and the next maintains the four basic subject areas but also attempts to discuss them in a unitive and interpretive manner, so that the four areas are drawn into an argumentatively conjoined three-part model of biblical-historical foundations plus two forms of contemporary application. The discussion that follows is intended to provide, not a traditional "theological encyclopedia," but a fundamentally historical interpretive path *through* the biblical and historical disciplines toward contemporary formulation. The genius of theology in the Judeo-Christian tradition has always been the fact that the tradition set in the context of a living community of belief provides the clearest and surest trajectory into the future.

HISTORY, CANON, AND CRITICISM

Christian faith begins both historically and functionally or existentially in the Bible and meditation on it. As Dietrich Ritschl has recently noted, theology, in the technical sense, "is unnecessary for the existence of belief grounded in the Bible" but necessary "in practice . . . because of the complications of our history."[1] The interpretive study of theology properly begins in Scripture and moves forward through these "complications of our history" in order to understand the way in which Scripture addresses us and is interpreted today.

The study of Scripture, Old Testament and New Testament, can be divided fairly neatly into linguistic, historical-exegetical, and theological elements. The basic issues and basic methods belong to both fields—and, indeed, to the historical study of Christianity in its development after the era of the New Testament. What I argue here for the use of Hebrew and Greek, for the application of historical method, and for the examination of theological issues will apply also to the discussion of church history and its place in the contemporary study of theology: the methods are the same, only the languages differ.

---

[1]Dietrich Ritschl, *The Logic of Theology: A Brief Account of the Relationship Between Basic Concepts in Theology* (Philadelphia: Fortress, 1986), p. 298.

By linguistic study I do not mean the rather perfunctory exercise of working through a grammar book. That, of course, is presupposed. Rather, by linguistic studies I mean the essentially interpretive task, based on grammatical study, of using the biblical languages as tools, as means of entry into the thought-world of the text. This very basic linguistic exercise is, moreover, both a hermeneutical task and, in the context of seminary and church, an element of spiritual formation. On the one hand, acquaintance with the way in which a language constructs its world and conveys its meaning is necessary to understanding the biblical view of God. The Old Testament conception of God as transcendent and immanent, trans-historical but historically active, other than worldly yet personally involved cannot be grasped unless our contemporary God-language is challenged and superceded, in exegesis, by an understanding not just of words and phrases taken over from the Old Testament and placed into our own language but of the way in which the reality of the divine is expressed in the language of the Old Testament itself. On the other hand, this new understanding of the language of the Old Testament in and for itself in its original context becomes an avenue for the development and formulation of our own understanding of the divine—specifically in and through the recognition that our own linguistic forms can be transcended and our conception of God enriched and expanded.

These comments on language must not be construed as an advocacy of the claim that we are, today, victims of a Greek or Latin view of God that has somehow replaced the Hebraic conception simply because of the conceptual framework inherent in these languages. In other words, nothing metaphysical or theological is inherent in a language that either demands or precludes certain forms of understanding. "Hebraic thinking" does not yield up a dynamic, concrete, personally related notion of God because of inherent linguistic necessities any more than "Greek" or "Latin thinking" yields up a static abstract, uninvolved notion of a divine Prime Mover. In addition, we need to recognize that the absence of certain ideas from the Hebrew mind as we know it from the Bible does not falsify those ideas. If this were so, biblical study would not enrich and expand our understanding; it would only replace our modern patterns of understanding conditioned as they are by the course of Western civilization, Hebraic, Hellenistic, and Latinate forms of expression, philosophies that use and transcend these linguistic forms, social perceptions and scientific achievements, and so forth, with an ancient pattern of understanding out of sympathy with, and perhaps unable to communicate with, our present cultural context. Linguistic study ought to open doors, not close them.[2]

Specifically, linguistic study includes the vocabulary, grammar, and syntax of a language, with attention given to the way in which words function as signifiers or signs, as placeholders that bear meaning and are capable of sustaining a range of meaning; to the way in which phrases and figures of speech point toward meaning beyond the wooden, literal implication of words set in a particular order; and to the way in which the grammatical structure of a language, the tense-structure of its verbs, the declension of its nouns and adjectives and so forth, facilitates or does not facilitate the conveyance of meaning. We can understand these issues in terms of the sensitivities of a translator whose task is the transfer of meaning from one language to another. In moving from Greek or Latin into modern English, perhaps the greatest difficulty lying in wait for the translator is the elaborate structure of declensions in the classical languages—nouns, pronouns, verbs, and adjectives all receive their forms from their role in the grammar of a sentence. This structure is not difficult to learn, but it is difficult to represent in English, which retains little evidence of declension and in which word order determines the role of words in a sentence. Beyond this problem lies the fact that there is virtually never a perfect equivalence between a word in one language and the word used to translate it in another language.

---

[2]On the subject of linguistics and interpretation, see Moisés Silva, *God, Language and Scripture: Reading the Bible in the Light of General Linguistics*, Foundations of Contemporary Interpretation, vol. 4 (Grand Rapids: Zondervan, 1990).

Since virtually all of our theological concepts have a multilingual history—moving from Hebrew to Greek, from Greek to Latin, and from Latin to one or more modern languages, sometimes from one modern language to another— some acquaintance with the original languages of the Bible and of our theology is necessary if only for the sake of recognizing how ideas may shift in emphasis and in meaning when they cross linguistic frontiers and how the transmission and retention of a theological idea, as Christianity moves from one language and culture to another, is a delicate and difficult process. Study of the biblical languages, then, is itself a theological exercise that not only enables one to understand the Scriptures more fully but also clarifies and enriches one's understanding of theology.

By way of example, even a beginning knowledge of Hebrew will enable a person to see that Hebrew has no exact equivalents of the terms of Greek and Latin philosophical and theological anthropology—body, soul, and spirit. Indeed, the language of the Old Testament points us toward the recognition that the problem of dichotomistic (body-soul) and trichotomistic (body-soul-spirit) anthropologies is that they turn aspects or functions of the human being into "parts" standing over against one another. Thus, the word typically translated "soul," *nephesh*, more accurately is rendered "living being": it does not indicate a spiritual over against a corporeal reality, but a whole person, an organic unity. *Nephesh* can even, albeit rarely, refer to a corpse (cf. Lev. 21:11; Num. 6:6). At the very least, it cannot be understood as "soul" in a philosophical sense.

Linguistic foundations, however, no matter how much insight they provide, are only a preparation for historical and exegetical study. History provides the background for exegesis, and exegesis functions, at least in part, to uncover the history. If we have learned nothing other than this from the frequently jarring history of the critical study of the Bible since the Enlightenment, the result was well worth the travail. The exegesis of the patristic and medieval periods, and even of the Reformation period, was frequently determined by then-contemporary theological confession rather than by a clear sense of the original historical setting of the text. Thus, although it would be unwise to discard the Niceno-Constantinopolitan language of the Trinity on the basis of the most recent critical commentary on the Johannine prologue, it would also be utterly foolhardy to examine the Johannine prologue with the preconceived assumption that the *monogenēs* of John 1:14, 18 stands as a direct reference to the eternal intra-Trinitarian relations of the first and second persons of the Trinity rather than to the unique filial relation of Jesus, understood by John as the Logos made flesh, to the fatherly God of Israel and the church. From a strictly historical and linguistic point of view, the author of the gospel of John could not have known the language of Nicea and Constantinople, and the fathers who sat at those councils were dealing with words and terms that had developed in their meaning and significance since the time of John.

Even more problematic than such a reading of the New Testament is the Christological exegesis of the Old Testament: there can be no access to the meaning of "image of God" in Genesis 1:27 if the phrase is read out in terms of New Testament and church usage—where "image of God" refers either to Christ or to certain spiritual virtues in human beings. One major exegetical and linguistic study relates the word "image" (*tselem*) to the use of a royal seal or boundary marker to set forth the delegated power of a viceroy: thus the image according to which male and female are made is a mark of dominion over the earth, a sign of custodianship that correlates with the rest of the language of the verse.[3] Similarly, the reading of a text like Psalm 2:7, "You are my son; today I have begotten you," (RSV) in terms of an intra-Trinitarian begetting or even in terms of the New Testament application of the text to Christ (Heb. 1:5), if done as a primary level of interpretation,

---

[3]David Clines, "The Image of God in Man," in *Tyndale Bulletin* 19 (1968): 53–103; cf. Walther Eichrodt, *Theology of the Old Testament*, 2 vols. (Philadelphia: Westminster, 1967), 2:122–31, where Eichrodt emphasizes the "special character" of the human being in relation to God as the central implication of the text.

can only obscure the relationship between God and the king of Israel described in this psalm of enthronement.

Historical and exegetical study of the materials in both testaments cannot simply follow an analytical or "critical" pattern of "divide and conquer." It is both to the credit and to the condemnation of much biblical scholarship that it has focused on the basic forms and pericopes of the text—to its credit because this procedure has enabled us to learn so much more about the context, the culture, and the history of the ancient world and about the text itself in the discrete elements that together contribute to its meaning, and to its condemnation insofar as this procedure has banished consideration of the whole of the literature in its final forms as the vehicle of greater and more enduring meaning than any particular pericope. Exegetical and historical study, as recent advocates of canonical criticism have argued, is incomplete until it has asked the larger questions. A similar point has been made by advocates of rhetorical criticism.[4]

Once the form, source, redaction, and textual critical work has been done, the final form of the text—the canonical form—in its literary and rhetorical unity must be considered. It is, for example, one thing to examine the text of Genesis and, as Jewish and Christian exegetes down through the centuries have done, to ponder the differences between the creation account that runs from Genesis 1:1 to 2:4a and the creation account that runs from Genesis 2:4b to 2:25, and quite another thing to leave one's readers or hearers with the impression that the two accounts pose an insoluble problem for the modern reader—as if the differences were obvious to us and not to the writer of Genesis. However one explains the juxtaposition of the two accounts, one is also bound to explain their presence in the canonical form of the Book of Genesis. These two tasks,

---

[4]On these issues and for a discussion of various kinds of criticism, see Tremper Longman III, *Literary Approaches to Biblical Interpretation*, Foundations of Contemporary Interpretation, vol. 3 (Grand Rapids: Zondervan, 1987); for a careful approach to "critical" method, see also Edgar Krentz, *The Historical-Critical Method* (Philadelphia: Fortress, 1975).

moreover, are not at all mutually exclusive. Once critical reading has pointed to the juxtaposition of different accounts, the theological task must begin. That task includes determining not only the theological meaning of each account but also, as canonical and rhetorical criticism demand, the theological significance of the juxtaposition itself and of the larger view of creation in relation to the narrative of beginnings in the first eleven chapters of Genesis.

The purpose of this critical and historical approach to Scripture is to place us as readers of the text into the milieu of the authors. We need to learn to read the text from its own point of view if we are ever to bring it to bear on our own context. After all, apart from what we may conclude from our doctrine of inspiration about the perpetual and perennial importance of the text, the biblical authors did not write with the later history of the Christian church in mind. They wrote in order to address the religious needs of particular communities at particular points in time. The critical and historical method ought to serve us by opening up the meaning of the text to us.

As G. B. Caird has pointed out, "It is a common modern fallacy that the development of scientific knowledge"—and, I add, critical method—has "made Christianity harder to accept." From the very first, as the apostle Paul wrote, Christianity was "a stumbling block to Jews and foolishness to Gentiles" (1 Cor. 1:23). "Only if," writes Caird, "we have the skill and the patience to discover why the gospel was a shock to man of the first century, shall we be able to use it to shatter the complacency and lift the vision of our own generation."[5]

As a final point in this section, we address the problem of canon. If, as I have argued from the outset of this study, the understanding of Christianity made possible through a cohesive and constructive study of theology and the development, out of this understanding, of adequate theological formulations are both religious and historical issues, then the broader issues raised by the history of the Judeo-Christian religious commu-

---

[5]G. B. Caird, "The New Testament," in *The Scope of Theology*, ed. Daniel T. Jenkins (Cleveland: World, 1965), p. 54.

nity come to bear on the critical discussion of Scripture most clearly and pointedly when we address the question of the canon of Scripture. The canon as we use it today is a dogmatically constituted document that was written and subsequently collected and defined over the course of the centuries. It neither represents the entire religious experience of ancient Israel and the earliest church nor expresses in its existence as canon the intentions of the biblical authors for the future use of their writings. There were quite a few documents produced by Jews and Christians during the canonical periods of their history that are not included in the canon, and the authors of the books presently in our canon did not produce those writings for the sake of their inclusion in the canon of Scripture! The canon was identified through the efforts of later generations to codify and regularize the religious traditions of the community.[6]

Although we do not have a body of ancient Israelite religious literature that stands outside of—either prior to or alongside—the Old Testament canon, there are references in the canon itself to books used as sources, like the Book of Jashar or the Book of the Wars of Yahweh, and there are also references to religious pronouncements that did not become canonical, like the prophecies of Hananiah and Shemiah. More importantly, the close of the Old Testament canon represents, in large part, a linguistic decision associated rather vaguely with the experienced end of prophecy. The writings that belong to the Apocryphal or Deuterocanonical scriptures are not in classical Hebrew or even in the Aramaic that appears in portions of Daniel, but in Greek. These writings represent, in part, a shift from prophecy to apocalyptic, but they also represent a continuation of the historical narrative of the Jewish people and of the wisdom tradition. The final, doctrinal exclusion of these books from the canon occurred only with the beginnings of Protestantism in the sixteenth century, and the decision to

---

[6]A significant approach to this problem of the creation of canon is found in H. N. Ridderbos, *Redemptive History and the New Testament Scriptures* (Phillipsburg, N.J.: Presbyterian and Reformed, 1988).

exclude the Apocrypha was not at all so easily made as the decision to exclude the second-century Gnostic witness to Jesus.

There are, moreover, noncanonical writings of the New Testament era that do stand in close relation not only to the New Testament but also to themes and doctrines resident in the Christian tradition. Writings such as the Similitudes of Enoch and IV Ezra, the Shepherd of Hermas, the Didache, and the Apocalypse of Peter left their mark on later Christianity— perhaps most noteworthy here is the enormous importance of the Apocalypse of Peter for the patristic and medieval pictures of what may be called "the geography of hell." There are also works, like the so-called Epistle of Paul to the Laodiceans, that faded in and out of the canon throughout the Middle Ages.

Since the identification of the canon of Scripture was not a historical-critical but a traditio-normative activity accomplished from within the community of belief, we can make a firm distinction between our historical and critical use of noncanonical documents for the better understanding of documents within the canon and our own theologically constructive use of only those documents that are in the canon. In other words, the historically blurred edges of the canon—like the historically blurred edges of the community—cannot become the basis for adopting a new and wider set of doctrinal norms than those established by the believing community with increasing precision during its long history. We cannot undo the early church's decision to exclude the Gnostic scriptures nor, as Protestants, can we undo the Reformers' decision to exclude the Deuterocanonical books from the Old Testament. All that has been preserved can be edifying, but only the canon can be doctrinally normative.

I say this so pointedly because of the recent tendency among some writers to have recourse to the Gnostic scriptures as an alternative trajectory for Christian doctrine and as a basis for developing a theological critique of the fathers of the first five centuries. Whereas the thought of the fathers must be understood in the context of such alternative trajectories, it remains true that contemporary Christianity rests on the thought of the fathers and their successors rather than on the alternative doctrinal perspective. The canon of Scripture, as the church now possesses it, partakes of the necessary particularity—indeed, of what some have called "the scandal of particularity"—of our religion. It is not within our ability to alter the past or to remove from our religion those characteristics that make it uniquely what it is. (I will make much the same point when we come to the issue of comparative religion and the history of religions.)

THE OLD TESTAMENT

Biblical study must provide the foundation for Christian theology, and Old Testament study is foundational to the understanding of the Bible. Separate study of the Old Testament apart from prior considerations grounded either in the New Testament or in the history and doctrine of the church is a relatively new phenomenon—newer even than Gabler's identification of a separate biblical theology. Of course, the Christian community regarded what we now call the Old Testament as Scripture before there was a New Testament, and the Old Testament has remained a primary source for Christian doctrines—the primary source for doctrines not directly bound to the order of salvation established in Christ and of doctrines, like covenant, that provide a context for understanding the offer of redemption in Christ. Historical understanding, particularly the historical understanding of the way in which teachings of the religious community (whether Israel or the church) arise and develop, however, demands that the chronological priority of the Old Testament be taken seriously as a foundation and ground-point of interpretation. For a right understanding of the religion of ancient Israel, the Old Testament must be studied separately—what is more, the separation is necessary for the right understanding of the New Testament as well.

The first and the most profound issue that we must address on our way from study of the Old Testament to the formulation of contemporary theology, then, concerns the relationship of the Old Testament to Christianity and the character of the Christian right to the theological traditions of ancient Israel that belong to the Old Testament. Very much as we propose to answer the larger question of the unity of the disciplines and of the character of theological formulation, and in fact as a part of that larger problem, we can look for a resolution of this issue along historical lines. The New Testament itself and its theological center, the work of Jesus of Nazareth, can hardly be understood in isolation from the history and religion of Israel and, specifically, from the history of the Jewish people in the centuries immediately preceding the time of Jesus. As many writers have pointed out, the history of the Jewish people, as recounted in the Old Testament and the intertestamental literature, is a theological and a theologized history. The work of God in and through the history of Israel provides the foundation for understanding the New Testament's approach to the work of God for Israel and for the nations in Jesus Christ.

This is not to say that the Old Testament is simply a background to the New. It is the normative account of the religion of Israel—and, therefore, of the religion of Jesus. It is a major error of interpretation to claim that the Old Testament is law without gospel and the New Testament gospel without law. The message of obedience to God flows through the whole of Scripture and cannot be understood in the church apart from the Old Testament statement of the law and the prophetic meditation on it. The message of salvation, similarly, belongs to the whole of Scripture and can hardly be grasped apart from the Old Testament meditation on the promise given to Israel. Indeed, without the Old Testament, the corporate character of religion, of obedience, and of grace, would be greatly obscured. This has occurred in churches that deemphasize the Old Testament, view it as background, separate the history of the church from the history of Israel, and believe that the Old Testament adds little to the New Testament message of repentance, faith, justification, and sanctification.

By making the point in this way, I intend to disagree with Ebeling's ordering of the disciplines—New Testament before Old Testament—and with his initial claim that "the pathway through the theological disciplines begins with the study of the

New Testament."[7] Wle it is obviously true that Christianity itself exists because of the events recorded and the revelation proclaimed in the New Testament, it is also true, though perhaps not so obviously, that it is dangerous to read the Old Testament as if it stands interpretatively subordinate in all its statements to the New Testament. It is equally dangerous to read the New Testament apart from the theological foundation provided in the earlier meditations of God's people, principally the writings contained in the canonical Old Testament. If we look forward to the discussion of systematic theology, we ought to be prepared to recognize that the great body of "Christian doctrine," like the New Testament itself, however much it is illuminated by the revelation of God in Christ, is drawn from the Old Testament. This foundational character of the Old Testament is evident in the doctrines of God, creation, providence, human nature, the fall, sin, and the covenant, that is, the doctrines placed traditionally at the beginning or in the first half of a theological system, doctrines that set the stage and provide the interpretative foundation, both theological and anthropological, of all that follows.

These introductory comments indicate a sharp rejection of the virtually Marcionite position of modern Christianity that refuses to consider the Old Testament as a proper text for preaching and theology and gravitates toward certain New Testament texts as a "canon within the canon." They indicate also an equally sharp rebuttal of the essentially allegorical method of reading the Old Testament that passes for theology under the term "Christocentrism." The Old Testament can speak to theology only if it is permitted to speak on its own terms as a foundational element of the theological curriculum and as a field of study in its own right. The Old Testament can be of genuine service to Christianity only if it is studied critically as a pre-Christian and, therefore, to a certain extent non-Christian body of literature.

It is not only a disservice to Old Testament exegesis but

---

[7]Gerhard Ebeling, *The Study of Theology*, trans. Duane Priebe (Philadelphia: Fortress, 1978), p. 13.

also a disservice to the history of Christian doctrine and to contemporary theology both systematic and practical to include Trinitarian considerations in the basic interpretation of Genesis chapter 1 or Christological considerations in the primary exegetical reading of the "Servant Songs" in Isaiah. On the one hand such a procedure would render the meaning of the text inaccessible to the text's own author and prejudice the modern interpreter against the original and basic meaning of the text. On the other hand the procedure conceals the interpretive efforts of succeeding generations—some of them following the close of the canon—to draw the text forward, in view of its original meaning, into the framework of meaning then characteristic of the community of belief.

From an initial, historical point of view, the Old Testament is the remaining literature of ancient Israel that surveys the history and religion of the Jewish people. In its variety, the Old Testament offers historical narratives, religious and ethical codes, preaching and prophecy, prayers, liturgies, and ancestral traditions, all of which existed in oral form prior to the writing of the text as we have it today. Beginning in the eighteenth century with Jean Astruc's *Conjectures on the Reminiscences which Moses Appears to Have Used in Composing the Book of Genesis* (1753), scholars have recognized that older sources underlay the final form of the books of the Old Testament, but it wasn't until 1835 with the appearance of Wilhelm Vatke's *Religion of the Old Testament* that these perceptions of earlier sources were united with a historical, developmental insight into a view of the historical course of the religion of the Old Testament. Although Vatke's views on the chronology and development of Old Testament religion have been greatly modified, his emphasis on a historical and developmental model for the study of the Old Testament remains with us. This is true of "conservative" as well as "liberal" discussion of the religion of the Old Testament—of Geerhardus Vos as well as Gerhard von Rad. The historical study of the Old Testament demands an openness to the past reality of Israelite religion and permits, in the second place, a more surefooted use of the Old Testament, as better understood, in the contemporary teaching of the church.

It is one of the great demerits of much modern Christianity, both nominally "conservative" and nominally "liberal," that it tends to ignore the Old Testament in its preaching and in its daily life, except for the occasional reference to the Decalogue and the Psalms. We need to be reminded continually that the greater part of the body of Christian doctrine rests on the Old Testament—and that the doctrine taught by Jesus had the Old Testament as its primary point of reference. As the Protestant theologians of the sixteenth and seventeenth centuries well recognized, the Old Testament records the life of the people of God and offers counsel and example to the church for all seasons.

The historical and theological understanding of the Old Testament has, in the last century, been enhanced by archaeological, literary, and linguistic study of the ancient Near East. Each of these areas of study is so specialized that theological students, ministers, and theologians cannot be expected to have a grasp of current scholarship or of all known documents—even documents in translation. Nonetheless, a general knowledge of these fields is so crucial to an understanding of Scripture that anyone attempting to formulate theology today must have an appreciation of the results of archaeology and of the literary and cultural study not only of Israel but also of her neighbors.

We cannot, for example, continue to make simplistic comments about the dynamic, concrete view of the world held by Israel and the Semitic nations over against the static, abstract approach of the Greeks or about the uniqueness of Israel's view of God acting in a linear history over against the presumed cyclic approach to history found in the thought of Israel's neighbors. Not only have the typical Hebrew/Greek dichotomies been shown, by linguists like James Barr, to be lacking in any foundation in the biblical languages themselves,[8] but also a very important essay by Bertil Albrektson has demonstrated that "the Old Testament idea of historical events as divine revelation must be counted among the similarities, not among

---

[8]James Barr, *The Semantics of Biblical Language* (London: Oxford University Press, 1961).

the distinctive traits: it is part of the common theology of the ancient Near East."[9]

We can, however, learn about the distinctive character of Old Testament theology on a considerably more detailed and significant level through the careful use of such cultural comparisons. Thus the biblical and the Babylonian creation narratives, despite their enormous differences, share several significant features. It is not at all accidental that the primal chaos, the *tehom*, of Genesis 1:2 is divided by God and held back by a firmament and that the chaos deity, *Tiamat*, of the Babylonian narrative is divided by the victorious Marduk and formed into earth, sea, and heavenly vault. The worldviews, indeed, the religious worldviews of Israel and her neighbors were similar. From these similarities, but also from the differences between the narratives, we learn how the fundamental monotheism of Israel interpreted and, in effect, demythologized the world-order. In Israel's account there is no cosmic battle between gods, and the primal chaos is not some divine being set in contrast to the one true God of heaven and earth. In its ancient Near Eastern context, Genesis 1:1-2:4a becomes more than just a statement concerning the origins of the world-order—a profound monotheistic manifesto against all forms of polytheism or dualism, uttered in the face of opposing religious beliefs. We find, in such a passage and in our critical perception of its meaning, an important element in and for the contextualization of Christianity today—not only in view of cults in the Western world but also in view of the polytheism and virtual polytheism that surrounds Christianity in Third World cultures.

We are also in a far better position to understand both the dangers and pressures of religious syncretism and the prophetic attack on the inroads of Canaanite religion when we have some access to the common elements between Yahwism and Baalism as well as to the differences. The cyclic character of worship associated with the agricultural life of Canaan was not foreign

[9]Bertil Albrektson, *History and the Gods: An Essay on the Idea of Historical Events as Divine Manifestations in the Ancient Near East and in Israel* (Lund: Gleerup, 1967), p. 114.

to Israelite worship and, indeed, the covenantal offering of firstfruits became in Canaan an integral part of Israelite worship. The Canaanite word *Baal*, moreover, was the equivalent of one of Israel's most cherished names for God, *Adonai*: both mean "Lord." It is not at all difficult to see how Israelites might be tempted to adopt some of the features of Canaanite religion, particularly in view of their adoption of agriculture when they settled in Canaan. Here again, the issue is not the direct use of materials but the application of principle: what we learn from the study of the text in its historical and cultural context becomes a basis for understanding the religious mind of the present as Christianity in America confronts other religions in the conduct of daily life.

One final comment: in addressing the Old Testament theologically as one element in the larger work of theological formulation in the present, we must never allow our present-day concerns to overrule the need to interpret the Old Testament on its own terms, but equally so, we must never allow our recognition of the necessity of interpreting the Old Testament on its own terms to negate our commitment to drawing it into our theological present. In fact, these two concerns ought not to stand against each other in conflict. I have tried to argue throughout this chapter, and throughout this entire volume, that historical understanding is the foundation for theological understanding. The Old Testament, we must always remember, presents to us a past reality. Scripture presents us, not, as Barth commented, with a "strange new world," but with a strange *old* world, a world that is mediated to us and given its present significance by a historical tradition of use and a historical pattern of interpretation.[10]

Inasmuch, moreover, as the Old Testament is the representation of the religious life of ancient Israel, not of ancient Christianity, our historical and theological approach to its literature needs to consider not only the meaning of the great transition from Old Testament to New Testament and the early

---

[10]Cf. Karl Barth, *The Word of God and the Word of Man*, trans., with a new foreword, by Douglas Horton (New York: Harper & Row, 1957), pp. 28–50.

church but also the ongoing life of Israel itself. I began this section by stating the priority of the Old Testament over the New Testament even in the Christian context and by insisting on the need to interpret the Old Testament without doctrinal preconditions dictated by the New Testament or by the early church. I close it by noting the need of Christian exegetes to respect and reckon with the work of Jewish exegetes and the need of Christian theologians to recognize both the common right of the two religious communities to the same literature and the shared exegetical and hermeneutical tradition that did not cease with the close of the canon. In moving, legitimately, from the Old Testament to the New Testament, the primary theological issue that we address is the way in which our tradition, the Christian tradition, has taken up these materials into its ongoing history and has reinterpreted them and imparted new significance in the light of successive stages in the life of our community. The existence of another community of faith, grounded in the same literature, does not challenge the present existence of our community of faith, but it does provide an important limit to our interpretation of that literature.

The historical model for theological formulation establishes the religious unity of the disciplines by recognizing that religion is a historical phenomenon and that therefore the interpretation of religion is a forward-moving historical process. Doctrinal statements that are legitimate readings of the past in the present life of the community cannot be pressed into the past as if they had arisen in that past historical context. Old Testament exegesis and Old Testament theology are rooted in the history of the religion of ancient Israel, not in the history of Christian doctrine or in systematic theology. Such an understanding of the task is crucial, moreover, not only to the integrity of the study of the Old Testament but also to the study—and the unified use in contemporary theological formulation—of the other disciplines.

THE NEW TESTAMENT

New Testament studies lie at the heart if not exactly at the beginning of the theological enterprise. It is therefore crucial that these studies be constructed and directed with a clear definition of their focus and boundaries. As we have already seen, "New Testament" identifies a body of literature that is historically vague but doctrinally or dogmatically precise. The New Testament does not stand in a vacuum nor can it be understood as the second of two books that God once wrote. The New Testament is a theologically and canonically defined body of literature that is preceded historically by an unbroken stream of writings extending from the Old Testament through the so-called intertestamental period, and followed historically by an unbroken stream of writings extending from the last book of the New Testament down to the present. In addition, this stream of writings from the Old Testament through the intertestamental, New Testament, patristic, medieval, Reformation, and modern periods, contains "trajectories" of ideas and writings that pass through the New Testament period without contributing to the New Testament: the Mishnah and the Talmud contain the living Jewish tradition that links the Old Testament canon to the present day for Judaism.

Crucial, therefore, to an exegetical and theological understanding of the New Testament is the continuance of the historical model introduced in our discussion of the Old Testament. The way in which biblical religion moves through the New Testament is nearly as important to Christian self-understanding as the unique language and teaching of the New Testament. Not only is it true that all documents must be understood in relation to their background and context, it is also true that the meaning of the New Testament witness belongs to the religion of an ongoing religious community that has existed both before and after the New Testament itself. The New Testament is both a contributor to the religious tradition of the community of belief and a bearer of it. Study of the New Testament, thus, must be guided by a sense of history, particularly by a sense of the history of the community of belief and of the role of the New Testament in that history.

The earliest Christian community existed within the bounds of Judaism and, together with other religious groups within Judaism—Pharisees, Sadducees, Essenes—shared the great tradition of the Old Testament and the intertestamental literature while also interpreting that tradition in its own way, in the light of the revelation of God in and through Jesus of Nazareth. Our theological approach to the writings of the New Testament must, therefore, be aware of the continuities and discontinuities of belief between the various religious groups. It is significant, for example, to our understanding of Jesus' conflict with the Pharisees that he stood closer to them than to the Sadducees: Jesus and the New Testament authors shared with the Pharisees a doctrine of the final glorious resurrection of the dead, a doctrine denied by the Sadducees on the ground of a strict reading of the Torah.

Similarly, our theological understanding and our theological use of the New Testament ought to be guided by a recognition of the broader context of the New Testament in the emerging Christian religion and, more generally, in the Graeco-Roman world. The early Christian community, as is easily seen in the Pauline epistles, included groups and teachers whose doctrines would not become normative and would receive only a negative reference in the New Testament. Gnostic and docetic beliefs seem to have been held in Corinth and, somewhat later (as testified by 2 Corinthians), a Judaizing tendency manifested itself in the same place, perhaps similar to, though not identical with, the Judaizing tendency in Galatia. The Gnostic tendency represents a contact between Christianity and a religious phenomenon broader than Judaism, whereas the so-called Judaizing tendency represents the original context of the Christian message in conflict with emerging Christianity, in the persons of some of the earliest converts. All of these variant readings belong to earliest Christianity, to its attempt to identify and interpret the significance of Jesus of Nazareth and his work—and all are important to our understanding of the meaning of the gospel and of the way it was formulated by Paul over against these various alternatives.

Outside of the Christian community, moreover, stood other religious traditions and practices that also colored the way in which the New Testament states its teachings and conditioned the way in which the gospel was received by the pagan population of the empire. Thus our theological understanding of the New Testament must include some acquaintance with the mystery religions of the ancient world with their blood-baptisms into life eternal and their foundational myths of a dying and rising god. Whereas teachings about baptism and resurrection were rejected in certain quarters of the Jewish community, such teachings were in fact welcomed by many pagans who could be attracted to Christianity on the basis both of this seeming common ground and of the ethical superiority of Christianity to these other religious options. In other words, we can begin to understand the success of the gentile mission in part on the grounds of the ability of the gentile world to grasp, albeit at a superficial level, some of the basic teachings of the church. The New Testament was, particularly in its Pauline expression, capable of cross-cultural transmission and contextualization.

These historical issues and the problems they raise for interpretation stand in a constant tension with the doctrinally and dogmatically precise canon of the New Testament in which we have the closest and clearest witness to Jesus Christ as Savior and Redeemer, which is to say, the genuine apostolic witness. This statement is, of course, a theological judgment reflecting the judgment of the early church. It must, in fact, be a theological judgment inasmuch as the materials being considered are, in their very substance, theological. Any contrary judgment, such as, for example, the contemporary claim that there is a genuine Jesus-tradition in Gnostic sources of the second century,[11] is also a theological judgment. The objective and critical study of the New Testament in its first- and second-century context does not escape the realm of theological judgment—but the objective historical and theological consideration of the canon as we have it can and does clearly justify both the identification of the canon as apostolic and of the noncanonical witness to Jesus as belonging, as one scholar has commented, to a category of "the bizarre" in which "fantastic

[11]See James M. Robinson and Helmut Koester, *Trajectories Through Early Christianity* (Philadelphia: Fortress, 1971).

symbols, beautifully intricate myths, weird heavenly denizens, and extraordinary poetry" indicate both a certain element of common ground with ancient Judaism and Christianity and a vast divergence.[12]

Historical understanding, then, does not give us the canon of the New Testament, but it does offer a basis for grasping first historically and then theologically the significance of the canon. The canon of the New Testament, which provides us with the theological materials central to our Christian faith, is a highly selective set of documents that established the doctrinal bounds of Christianity and set in motion the central trajectory of the church's faith long before the church produced the full number of its creeds and dogmas. The documents within the canon, moreover, notwithstanding their profound agreement about the identity and meaning of Jesus Christ over against the views expressed in the noncanonical documents, do evidence considerable diversity.

The Synoptic Gospels are quite different in organization and somewhat different in content from one another. The gospel of John bears little resemblance to the synoptics. The Pauline writings speak differently of Jesus than do the Petrine and Johannine writings and the Epistle to the Hebrews. The chronology of the Pauline mission indicated by the Epistles is difficult (though not impossible) to reconcile with the book of Acts. The full significance of these writings in their diversity can be grasped only through a careful interpretation of their contents and context. (Without historical and critical understanding, the tendency to overlook the differences of approach and to find a theological common denominator—typical of later orthodox dogmatics—becomes all too easily the norm for interpretation, and the New Testament can no longer critique our theology.)

In the Pauline and Johannine literature we find, with the sole exception of the Epistle to the Hebrews, the most highly developed theologies of the New Testament, the former

---

[12]Bentley Layton, *The Gnostic Scriptures*, a new translation with annotations and introductions (Garden City: Doubleday, 1987), pp. xviii–xix.

representing an early stage of the Christian witness, predating
the final form of the Synoptic Gospels, the latter representing a
late first-century preaching, probably the latest theological
testament in the canon. In the movement from exegesis and
interpretation to theology, not only these differences—including both the differences in forms of speech arising from
different cultural or social contexts and the differences arising
from the development of Christian teaching—have to be
considered but also the ways in which those differences express
or address theological problems. And all of this has, as well as
possible, to be drawn into the contemporary situation. By way
of example: contemporary discussions of Christology need to
ask how the various and rather distinct ways of presenting the
divinity of Christ, from Pauline preexistence language to the
statements in Colossians that Jesus Christ is "the firstborn over
all creation" and that the "fullness" of the Godhead dwelt in
him (Col. 1:15, 19), to the Logos language of the Johannine
prologue and the Son language in the larger part of the gospel of
John, not to mention the various titles provided by the Synoptic
Gospels, point toward ways in which the church's proclamation
can be made to speak more directly to various cultures in the
world today. We live in an age when the traditional "person"
and "nature" language of the church has become increasingly
difficult to use, particularly because of the shift in the meaning
of the term *person* since the sixteenth century. Both theological
system and Christian proclamation need to take up the
challenge and reinvestigate the problem—not for the sake of
saying anything against the tradition that has served us so well
on this matter, but for the sake of doing as much justice to the
New Testament preaching of Christ in our time as the church
did in the first five centuries of its existence.

Similarly, the Synoptic Gospels, once viewed as a form of
biography, have yielded up to historical and critical study a
wealth of theology. As the medieval church easily recognized
for the gospel of John, the differences in arrangement of
materials in the gospels indicate, not a disagreement over the
strict chronology of Jesus' life, but differences of theological
perspective. This theological richness has been recovered for us

by analysis of the materials in the gospels with a view to their form and to the historical situation that produced them. At the very least, the Jewish Christian background of Matthew and probably of Mark can be contrasted theologically as well as stylistically with the Hellenistic perspective of Luke, with significant results. Matthew's Christology rests on the preaching of Christ as the new or second Moses, the One who fulfills and delivers the law of the new Israel. There may even be a parallel between the five major discourses in Matthew (chaps. 5–7; 10; 13; 18; 23–25) and the five books of the Law. Luke, however, as befits his Hellenistic context, takes a broader perspective and understands Christ as the center of salvation history. In both cases we are presented with theological perspectives that, like those noted above for Paul and John, can and ought to be developed in contemporary theology, both systematic and practical, as ways of moving the church of the present day forward into its own cultures with a message that is better adapted to the patterns and forms of expression characteristic of our times.

It is worth noting that Oscar Cullmann,[13] Johannes Munck,[14] Jürgen Moltmann,[15] and Wolfhart Pannenberg,[16] whose works many of us have found so engrossing theologically, precisely because they pressed us to reconsider the ways in which the biblical message could and ought to be stated in the present and precisely because their options for theological reconstruction seemed to speak so directly to the twentieth century, have all listened carefully to the ways in which the New Testament text, in its variety of forms, expressed the identity of Jesus of Nazareth and his role in the history of salvation. Cullmann and Pannenberg in particular have directed

[13]Oscar Cullmann, *Salvation in History*, trans. Sowers, et al. (London: SCM, 1967).

[14]Johannes Munck, *Paul and the Salvation of Mankind* (London: SCM/Atlanta: John Knox, 1977).

[15]Jürgen Moltmann, *Theology of Hope: On the Ground and Implications of a Christian Eschatology* (New York: Harper & Row, 1965).

[16]Wolfhart Pannenberg, *Jesus—God and Man*, trans. L. Wilkins and D. Priebe, rev. ed. (Philadelphia: Westminster, 1968).

our attention toward the historical as a fundamental biblical and theological category capable of being used in the present, granting that Western culture at least is gripped by its own historicity and that the category of history provides one way of understanding the interrelatedness of humanity throughout our world.

BIBLICAL THEOLOGY

Biblical interpretation is incomplete until it has addressed the history of Israel and its religion, the history of earliest Christianity and the development of its understanding of Jesus Christ, and the question of the theology of the Old and New Testaments. In other words, biblical study involves questions of the unity and larger implication as well as the diversity of the message, of the trajectory of biblical religion as well as the minute forms of the text. If this is the most difficult step in the process of biblical interpretation, it is also the most important one for the determination of the theological implications of the biblical message. It is, in other words, the theological link that joins biblical study to the other theological disciplines, just as historical consciousness is the broad methodological link.

It is worth noting here, if only for the purpose of setting aside the statement as useless, that all Christian theology is in some sense "biblical." Frequently systematic or dogmatic theologies will make the claim that they are writing or teaching "biblical theology." Their work is biblical because, in the spirit of traditional Protestantism, they look to Scripture as their primary norm for the statement of Christian doctrine. All well and good. But then these systems go on to discuss the divine essence and attributes by dividing the discussion into such categories as *attributa incommunicabilia* and *attributa communicabilia* or to derive the attributes by the *via negativa, via eminentiae,* and *via causalitatis.* They go on to structure their systems around such concepts as the *pactum salutis,* the *foedus gratiae,* the *foedus operum,* and the *ordo salutis.* At this point the "gentle reader" may well begin to wonder which Bible this systematic theolo-

gian has been reading.[17] I make the point with no intention of
impugning the value of the terms but only to point out that the
technical language of the divine attributes arose during the
Middle Ages, while the various terms for covenant (*pactum* and
foedus) did not appear in these forms before the sixteenth and
seventeenth centuries, and the much-valued dogmatic term for
"order of salvation" originated in the early eighteenth century.

How biblical is a "biblical theology" that takes its most
important terms and its major doctrinal topics from somewhere
other than the Bible? Even more importantly, how can we
formulate a theology that is at once cognizant of its biblical
roots and norms and capable of dealing with the doctrinal
categories that the church has developed over the course of
many centuries of meditation on its faith? A first step toward
the solution to these problems is to distinguish carefully
between biblical and systematic theology—to allow biblical
theology to address the religion of the Bible on its own terms
and to allow systematic theology to incorporate biblical
materials into a larger structure that acknowledges its biblical
foundation but also uses the tools provided by the church.

Biblical theology represents a crucial step in the interpretive enterprise that reaches from exegesis toward the contemporary theoretical and practical use of the materials of theology. In
order to understand just how crucial this step is, we must take a
brief look at the origins and the implications of this subdiscipline. Biblical theology did not exist as a distinct genre, in the
modern sense of the term, in the patristic, medieval, Reformation, or post-Reformation eras. Christian thinkers simply
assumed that their theology was "biblical" in the broadest sense
and that the step from exegesis to doctrinal statement or to
preaching was short and direct. This assumption was justified,
in large part, by exegetical and hermeneutical assumptions held

---

[17]And since my purpose was to note a problem for theology, I have no
intention of offering definitions for these terms here. Anyone desiring a
definition may consult Richard A. Muller, *Dictionary of Latin and Greek
Theological Terms, Drawn Principally from Protestant Scholastic Theology* (Grand
Rapids: Baker, 1985).

in the so-called precritical eras of the church's history. The beginnings of historical consciousness and of textual, critical study of Scripture in the sixteenth and seventeenth centuries led to a shift away from the allegorical exegesis of the Middle Ages to a more literal, grammatical, and historical emphasis. At the same time, beginning in the seventeenth century, Protestant theologians like Hermann à Diest and Sebastian Schmid recognized, in a rudimentary way, the need for a step between exegesis and system, a gathering of texts related to particular doctrinal concerns into a compendium of biblical doctrine. These compendia they called "biblical" theologies.

In the eighteenth century, under the impact of historical method and the rising sense of the historicity of knowledge itself, biblical scholars and theologians developed the category of "biblical theology" into a discipline in its own right—so that it was no longer a mere gathering of texts in support of and governed by the topics and methods of dogmatic theology, but instead a study of the theology of Scripture itself, governed by a historical understanding of the biblical materials themselves. Although several Bible scholars had produced critiques of the older biblical theologies and had attempted to write strictly textual expositions of the doctrines of the Bible without recourse to the historical expression of the church's doctrines prior to Johann Philipp Gabler's effort, his address "On the Proper Distinction between Biblical and Dogmatic Theology" (1787) marks the beginning of a conscious methodological distinction between the theological examination of biblical concepts in their own historical setting and development and the construction of a churchly dogmatics.

The theological encyclopedists of the nineteenth century recognized the methodological problem of dealing with this new discipline of "biblical theology." Schleiermacher, who valued exegetical theology highly, doubted the usefulness of a separate discipline of "biblical dogmatics" as developed in his day and placed it, together with church polity and symbolics, under the larger category of "historical knowledge of the present condition of Christianity," as a kind of adjunct to dogmatic theology proper.[18] (Note that Schleiermacher viewed exegetical theology, church history, and dogmatics together as forms of "historical theology.") Hagenbach, who presented theology in a strict fourfold model, followed Gabler's definition and included "biblical dogmatics" under the rubric "historical theology," while Schaff, recognizing on the one hand that the Bible itself is not a theological system and on the other that "biblical theology" is a systematization of exegetically gathered materials, placed it into the field of "systematic theology" and defined it as "the first and fundamental form of Didactic Theology, on which ecclesiastical and philosophical dogmatic and Ethic must rest throughout."[19]

This older problem of the methodological placement of the discipline is reflected today in the debate over the shape and method of biblical theology. It is generally recognized that such a theology must deal either with the Old Testament or with the New Testament and certainly not with a synthesis of the materials of the two testaments. The historical differences between the individual books of the Bible together with the historical development of the teaching of both the Old Testament and the New Testament as distinct disciplines stands in the way of a synthetically arranged theology of the whole Bible or a dogmatically organized theology of either testament. In addition, it is clear that the topics of a modern dogmatic system cannot be legitimately imposed on the text of Scripture (just as they cannot be legitimately imposed on the theological materials of the patristic period). Thus the older dogmatic models for biblical theology, like A. B. Davidson's *Theology of the Old Testament* or Van Oosterzee's *Theology of the New Testament*, no matter how insightful their comments on individual texts or on larger points of biblical teaching, are viewed—and rightly so—as methodologically unacceptable. These strictures apply even to Vriezen's brilliant *Outline of Old Testament Theology*. Despite

---

[18]Friedrich Schleiermacher, *Brief Outline on the Study of Theology* (Atlanta, Ga.: John Knox, 1966), pp. 86–87.

[19]Cf. Crooks and Hurst, *Theological Encyclopedia*, pp. 310–11 with Schaff, *Theological Propaedeutic*, pp. 316–17.

problems in establishing the date of books of the Bible, the historical method manifest in Eichrodt's and Von Rad's Old Testament theologies, Ringgren's *History of the Religion of Israel*, or Goppelt's *New Testament Theology* is preferable.

As even a cursory examination of these latter volumes will reveal, the historical concern that unites them also allows for considerable diversity and even disagreement in approach to the materials and the literature of biblical theology. Eichrodt's work, for example, holds in tension the methodological assertion that Old Testament theology is a historical and descriptive discipline with a thematic organization that maintains some points of resemblance to the older topical theological models of Old Testament theology and with a highly kerygmatic style of exposition that attempts to do justice to the revelatory character of Israelite religion. Von Rad, by way of contrast, totally avoids the thematic or topical approach and, in profound disagreement with Eichrodt, moves away from an attempt at theological synthesis to an examination of the historical lines of development of the different traditions within the Old Testament. Both, however, understand their quest for a central characteristic of the Old Testament—whether as in Eichrodt's case its theological, structural unity or in Von Rad's its traditionary tendencies—as the basis for pointing to what Eichrodt has called "the essential coherence" of the Old Testament with the New Testament.[20]

Another way of posing the issue of biblical theology is to note that although it is much easier to adapt to present-day use a "theology of the Old Testament" organized on doctrinal principles, it may be more useful to the understanding of the beliefs of the Old Testament to follow out a "history of the religion of Israel." Despite all the problems entailed upon the dating of the books of the Old Testament, the meaning, for example, of the words of the prophets on various provisions in the law, or of the many different accounts of the divine work of creation, can be more clearly and surely understood through a historically aware analysis of the purpose and setting of

---

[20]Eichrodt, *Theology of the Old Testament*, 1:31.

documents and parts of documents than through a theological harmonization. For example, Ezekiel's vision of the valley of dry bones (37:1–14) makes little sense apart from the knowledge that Ezekiel is an exilic prophet and that the bones of the slain represent the slain nation of Israel, then in captivity, but soon, like the dry bones, to be restored to life and health. Lacking a clear knowledge of or interest in the history of Israel, not a few past theologies have misread the passage as a prophecy of the final resurrection and have entirely lost the relationship between Ezekiel's preaching and the rest of the prophetic witness. The historical/theological point is, moreover, not simply a curiosity to be locked away in an erudite book: it has direct bearing on how the text of Ezekiel 37 can be used in the pulpit—and how it ought not to be used.

Another methodological issue should be noted: the history of religion model would have more interest in nonbiblical materials, the religions of surrounding peoples, and those teachings rejected by the canonical tradition of Israelite religion than would a theology of the Old Testament. This means that a history of the religion of Israel would tend to be more descriptive, whereas an Old Testament theology would tend to set forth a more normative presentation of the religious thought of ancient Israel. Eichrodt, for example, described the fundamental task of his theology as providing a topical cross-section of the thought of the Old Testament.[21] Nonetheless, as virtually all modern writers on the subject have acknowledged—largely because of the impact and importance of the study of the history of Israelite religion—these topics must reflect the faith of Israel, not the faith of the Christian church. The topics must be drawn from the religious life of Israel itself. This means, in turn, that the normative character of Old Testament theology (considered as a genre of theological writing) is a normative statement in and for the context of ancient Israel, recognized as normative in its ability to address the national religious experience of ancient Israel.

Significantly, this history of the religion of Israel (together

---

[21]Ibid., p. 28.

with a historically constructed theology of the New Testament) follows out a pattern and a method not unlike the history of Christian doctrine and, like the history of Christian doctrine, remains distinct from systematic theology. Understood in this way, the theology of the books of the Old Testament and the historically conceived theology of the Old Testament as a whole will have a cohesion and a clarity of meaning that can contribute to contemporary theology far more constructively than a dogmatically presented Old Testament theology. For one thing, the historical and methodological separation between biblical and systematic theology enables us to find a point for critiquing or developing our own theology that, without the separation, would have been unavailable. What is more, properly used, the historical insight can provide clues to what we will later discuss under the rubric of "contextualization."

The point is somewhat more difficult to make concerning New Testament theology, granting the place of the New Testament witness to Jesus Christ in Christian theology and the traditional Protestant sense of the immediate relationship between Christ and faith. This makes the point all the more important, however, with reference to the New Testament. Instead, for example, of approaching the New Testament with a strict definition of the order of salvation lined out neatly from election and calling to glorification, Christians ought to be in a position to allow the New Testament itself to govern directly the concept of an order of salvation, even to the point of asking whether such a concept can be constructed on the basis of the New Testament, out of an understanding of the meaning of the New Testament materials in their original context.

Of course, a historical approach to the theology of the New Testament must be profoundly compressed and far more attendant to minutiae than a similar approach to the Old Testament—and still more so than the historical study of the church's doctrines from the second century to the present. Periodization becomes exceedingly difficult, but clarity concerning the broad outlines of the religious and cultural milieu becomes easier to discern. It is also easier to organize a theology of the New Testament along historical lines than it is to organize a theology of the Old Testament. There is a general agreement about the order of composition of the gospels. Pauline chronology, although troublesome in some of its particulars, is clear in its general outlines: no one doubts that 1 Thessalonians is early Paul and Colossians is late—and this chronology has significant theological implications, as, for example, for the relationship of eschatology and ethics. The Johannine and Petrine literature separates out easily into distinct units, as does the Epistle to the Hebrews. Once these basic divisions are made, then such theological questions as the development of Christological formulae and the movement from Jesus' preaching of the kingdom to the earliest community's postresurrection preaching about Jesus as Christ and Lord can be opened for discussion and clarification.

Without appearing naïve about a hope for consensus among New Testament scholars on questions of date, authorship, and patterns of development, we can still look with some confidence to New Testament theology for a discussion of the meaning of Jesus of Nazareth to the earliest Christian community that is free from the encumbrances of later dogmatic language. And because it is free from these encumbrances, it is capable of becoming a basis for critiquing and formulating Christology meaningfully in the present. It is precisely because New Testament theology is not a discipline directed primarily toward a normative churchly statement of doctrine in the present that it can be a point of critique and a ground for new insight into contemporary theology.

Before we conclude this section, it is worth observing that the theological study of the New Testament shares the debate between a strict history of religion approach and a theological approach that we have noted previously with reference to Old Testament theology. The broad spectrum of approach is well evidenced in the recent works of Koester, Goppelt, and Schelkle. All feel it is important to understand the materials of the New Testament historically and all are aware of the religious environment of earliest Christianity and of the ways it impacted on the thought of the New Testament authors. Koester's *Introduction to the New Testament*, not strictly a theology, offers a foundational survey of earliest Christianity in its cultural context.[22] The entire first volume presents non-Christian materials: Greek and Roman religion, the oriental mystery religions, and later Judaism. When Koester approaches earliest Christianity in volume 2, he consciously avoids an exclusive emphasis on the canonical materials and includes the New Testament apocrypha and Gnostic sources in his analysis. The earliest Christian theology that Koester presents, therefore, is discussed entirely from the perspective of the history of religion, without any separation of canonical from noncanonical, "orthodox" from "heterodox" materials. The value of this approach is precisely that it manifests the early Christian experience as it might have appeared to its Hellenistic and Roman environment, where no neat distinction could be made between Christian orthodoxy and Christian heresy and where any distinction between canonical and noncanonical writings could be only anachronistically applied.

With Goppelt's eminent *Theology of the New Testament*, we enter a more traditional form of the discipline in which the historical perspective is applied to the discussion of the canonical New Testament. Goppelt states from the very outset of his first volume that "the New Testament is our only source of reliable traditions about the ministry of Jesus and the founding of the church and its proclamation."[23] Goppelt orients his work toward the views of the individual canonical writers with close attention to exegetical and historical issues, moving from a discussion of background and sources to the teaching of Jesus and on to Pauline and post-Pauline teaching. His approach is historical and essentially descriptive.

Schelkle's *Theology of the New Testament* adds a significant dimension to our discussion because it breaks with the trend in New Testament studies and follows an unabashedly systematic model. It begins with creation (world, time and history, and

[22]Helmut Koester, *Introduction to the New Testament*, 2 vols. (New York and Berlin: DeGruyter, 1982).

[23]Goppelt, *Theology of the New Testament*, trans., John Alsup, 2 vols. (Grand Rapids: Eerdmans, 1981–82), 1:xxv.

man), moves on to salvation history and revelation (including
Schelkle's Christology and doctrine of God), obedience, sin,
grace, and the virtues of Christian life gathered under the topic
of "morality," and concludes with a volume on church and
eschatology. Schelkle follows, nonetheless, a historical and
descriptive method that is concerned with the chronology of
earliest Christianity and, under each doctrinal topic, with the
movement of thought from the Old Testament and the
Hellenistic Jewish background, through the canonical writings
of the New Testament toward the writings of the postapostolic
period.[24] Schelkle is saved from most of the problems of the
older, dogmatic approach to New Testament theology by his
historical approach and by the fact that his broad doctrinal
categories are grounded and arranged, for the most part, on the
basis of his reading of the text rather than on the basis of
churchly dogmatics.

Although biblical theology defined and developed in this
independent, historical form has proved somewhat disconcerting to the dogmatic enterprise of some not merely conservative
but distinctly "old fashioned" modern-day theologians, this
newer view of the theology of Scripture ultimately proves to be
a positive development not only in the field of biblical study but
also in the construction of the other theological disciplines,
indeed, of the whole fourfold model for the study of theology.
When biblical theology is placed firmly into the biblical field
(and not into either the historical or the systematic fields), it
appears as the final exegetical task, conceived within the limits
of exegetical method but designed to draw biblical study
together by making sense of the whole. Biblical theology ought
to be the distillate of the exegete's labors—and, as such, it can
point directly toward the history of Christian doctrine, with
which it shares its historical-doctrinal method and outlook.
Moreover, together with the history of Christian doctrine, it
ought also to point critically and constructively toward contemporary systematic and practical theology *precisely because* it is

---

[24]Karl Hermann Schelkle, *Theology of the New Testament*, trans. William
Jurgens, 4 vols. (Collegeville, Minn.: Liturgical Press, 1971–78).

constructed biblically and historically without reference to the structures of churchly dogmatics.

Adolf Schlatter underlined this point in his epochal essay "The Theology of the New Testament and Dogmatics" (1909).[25] On the one hand, he declared that "the justification for a New Testament theology conceived as history is that the independent development of historical science gives a measure of protection, admittedly not infallible, against arbitrary reconstructions of its object." Schlatter was particularly concerned to avoid an intermixture of Scripture, churchly dogma, and personal theological opinion that would prevent both Scripture and dogma—not to mention personal opinion—from being "correctly grasped and fruitfully applied." "Conversely," Schlatter concluded, "the good conscience of the Christian dogmatician, and his ability to mediate effectively what the New Testament presents us with both to himself and the church, is partly dependent on the faithfulness and success with which we do our historical work on the New Testament."[26]

All of the historical and critical approaches—whether Koester's, Goppelt's, or Schelkle's—ought to have, therefore, an attractiveness to those who are presently involved in the study and formulation of Christian theology. Koester's history-of-religions approach, like the strict history-of-religions approach to the Old Testament, offers more religious materials from the first and second centuries than would probably find their way into a systematic or practical theological statement, even negatively as examples of paths that Christianity did not take. Nonetheless, the noncanonical and, by patristic standards, heterodox views of Jesus and of early Christian proclamation provided in the materials surveyed by Koester, manifest in clear relief the nature of the choices made by the early church in its identification of the genuine apostolic preaching. In the Gnostic *Acts of John*, for example, we encounter an argument for

---

[25]In *The Nature of New Testament Theology: The Contribution of William Wrede and Adolf Schlatter*, ed. and trans., with an intro., by Robert Morgan (Naperville, Ill.: Allenson; London: SCM, 1973), pp. 117–66.

[26]Ibid., p. 128.

docetism against the views of the canonical New Testament: here Jesus is portrayed as being human only in appearance, indeed, as changing his appearance at will—at times appearing as a child, at other times as a young man or as an old man with a beard, at times having a "hard," material body, at other times being "soft and immaterial and leaving no footprints."[27] The early church, by means of its identification of canonical writings and its application of an apostolic "rule of faith" not unlike our present-day Apostles's Creed, set aside this view and taught, as we see in the Synoptic Gospels, a fully human Jesus whose genuine humanity was necessary to the work of salvation. This point, manifest in extreme clarity by the contrast between the canonical and noncanonical writings, ought not to be lost on contemporary theological formulation. This is particularly true insofar as docetism, the claim that Jesus' humanity was mere appearance, remains a danger to the church's proclamation in our own times.

The other two approaches, whether the canonical, historical approach of Goppelt or the systematic approach of Schelkle, have a more direct impact on contemporary formulation, as does an Old Testament theology presented in the manner of Eichrodt's. In both cases, the trajectories of canonical teaching that are analyzed historically for their theological implications offer insight into the character and rationale of later churchly formulations and provide a foundation for the analysis and critique of systematic formulations and practical approaches in use today. From the point of view of present-day formulation, these theologies of the New Testament codify and present the results of exegesis to nonspecialists who are laity, clergy, and, potentially, specialists in other fields, such as the history of doctrine, systematic theology, or homiletics.

CHURCH HISTORY AND THE HISTORY OF DOCTRINE

Once we recognize the problem of the canon of Scripture and the problem (or question!) of our own relation to that canon

---

[27]Koester, *Introduction*, 2:197–98.

as a single and rather momentous hermeneutical question that cannot be answered solely from the side of the canon (inasmuch as we as church are responsible for the identification of the canon) or solely from the side of our own present (inasmuch as our present, understood theologically or religiously, has been constructed in the light of the canon and its previous interpretation)—then we are in a position to understand the relevance of church history and the history of doctrine both objectively and subjectively, hermeneutically and spiritually, to the study of theology. Church history and the history of doctrine provide the connecting link between us and the text. They belong to the hermeneutical circle in which the text is carried forward, interpreted, and shown to be significant in the present.

The separation of the biblical and the church historical disciplines, moreover, is a natural and necessary result of the church's self-understanding and of the way in which the various documents have affected and influenced the life of the community of belief. Farley's questioning of the fourfold curriculum and, by implication, of a particular way of doing theology on the basis of Scripture but in the light of an ongoing albeit less-normative tradition falls short of the mark. We do not have to invoke classic orthodox doctrines like the inspiration, infallibility, and divine authority of Scripture at this point: in the context of the question, such doctrines do not amount to proofs in any case. Instead, it is quite enough that we register the fact that the dogmatically defined canon of Scripture, even granting the different identifications of canon in the several great Christian communions, has had a qualitatively different effect and continues to have a qualitatively different effect on the consciousness of the community of belief than does the body of noncanonical documents. When we enter the realm of church history, we enter a portion of the Judeo-Christian tradition that functions differently in theology and in worship than the portion that belongs to the canon.

The danger presently confronting the study of church history and historical theology, as for the several biblical disciplines, is that they become fragmented into specialties defined by narrow areas of scholarly research rather than pointing, in their own way, toward the unity of theology as a whole. Here again, the importance of the survey—what in my own teaching I tend to characterize as "theology from Ignatius of Antioch to Pannenberg et al."—cannot be underestimated. No specialist can afford to forget that even the minutiae of research into the events of a few years in the twelfth century stand in relation to and, in fact, are illuminated by a broad knowledge of the larger whole of the life of the church in its history. This is not a matter of attempting to continue a biblical salvation history out into the life of the church or of making tradition a coequal norm with Scripture. Rather, it is a matter of recognizing the place of the larger flow of the history of the church and its teachings in the hermeneutical circle that links and binds us in the present to any and all other moments in that history—whether technically "biblical" or churchly—and conveys their significance to the present.

Some definition of the two disciplines is in order. It was typical of the nineteenth-century idealist approach to historical study to focus on the history of ideas as the focus of historical meaning. From that approach comes the still frequently heard definition of church history as the history of the institution of the church, including its doctrines, as it existed in relation to the culture of the world around it—and of the history of doctrine as the inward or interior history of the teachings of the church in their organic development. This definition does have the advantage of clearly showing church history to be the larger category that contains with it, among other things, the history of doctrine. It carries, however, the disadvantage and grave defect of severing events from ideas and giving the impression that "external history" is a husk ultimately discarded in the quest for inner, ideational reality. The opposite, however, is the case. Just as church history is the larger disciplinary category, so also is it the context within which the history of doctrine must be understood. Ideas do influence events, but the ideas themselves must be understood within their proper cultural, social, political, and intellectual setting inasmuch as the setting gives rise to and shapes the ideas.

Church history, then, is the larger investigation of the

corporate body of believers in its cultural, social, political, geographical, and intellectual context and in the development of its institutions, worship, mission, and intellectual and spiritual life. This investigation, moreover, must be undertaken critically, with the understanding that the history even of spiritual things is a history that is analyzed and explained in terms of the usual criteria of historical investigation. For example, it is doctrinally arguable to attribute the accurate preservation of the text of Scripture to divine providence inasmuch as Scripture contains the foundation of the church's preaching of salvation. Historical investigation cannot, however, rest content with the doctrinal explanation but must look to the process of the transmission of the text and examine the procedures and techniques of the Masoretes, the monastic calligraphers of the church, and the scholarly editors of later centuries, and find in the actual practice of these people the historical grounds for arguing whether or not the text has been accurately preserved. It also ought to be clear that, at least in our times, the historical investigation must precede the doctrinal statement and in fact supply the information from which the doctrinal statement takes its shape and on which it rests.

History of doctrine is the examination of the theological teachings of the church in their historical setting and their development. Like church history, the history of doctrine is an essentially analytical and descriptive discipline. Thus, in examining the teachings of Arius and the movement of doctrine toward Nicea, it is not the task of the historian of doctrine to evaluate in any ultimate sense the rightness or wrongness of Arius' views or of the response to Arius and Arianism made by the Council of Nicea and its defenders. Rather, the historian is committed to the precise exposition of Arius' theology, including the way in which it arose from and contributed to its cultural and intellectual context. Rightly or wrongly, Arianism had considerable power and appeal: it is the task of the historian to examine this appeal. The orthodoxy of Nicea must also be examined in its cultural and intellectual context—so that the forms of its doctrinal expression and their adequacy to the needs of fourth-century Trinitarianism can be fully understood. A dogmatic reading of the materials that assumes the rightness of Nicea on the basis of some contemporary orthodoxy will entirely miss the full significance of the council.

Church history, therefore, can hardly be studied without attention to the history of doctrine—inasmuch as the history of doctrine is an integral part of the social, cultural, institutional, and intellectual history of the church. And whether or not the whole is greater than the sum of its parts, it cannot be understood if one of the parts is omitted from the equation. History of doctrine, on the other hand, cannot be rightly studied in isolation from the larger history of the church. Its teachings—even at their most abstract—still reflect the churchly context out of which they arise. As we noted in the previous discussion of biblical theology, the method and organization of these disciplines arise out of historical and contextual concerns: like biblical theology, the history of doctrine cannot be constructed on systematic models drawn from the present. This was the great problem with the nineteenth-century histories of doctrine, such as those of Neander, Hagenbach, and Shedd. They all place a primary emphasis on doctrinal theology, Scripture, God, Creation, sin, and so forth—and they press each age of the church into a predetermined pattern. If we really wish to understand the past on its own terms and utilize our understanding in a critique of the present, the discussion of any period in history must rest on thought-categories drawn from that period. Only then, for example, can we see that the typical model of theological system did not begin to appear in the West until the twelfth century; whatever its validity, it does not arise directly out of the teaching either of Scripture or of the early church.

History of doctrine and church history both draw on churchly, confessional understandings and on general, methodological concepts held in common by ecclesiastical and secular historians. Church history and history of doctrine very naturally gravitate toward emphases and even periodizations of history that carry with them theological assumptions and judgments. Rather than view history as merely chronology—a list of "one thing after another" with no interpretive statement of relationship or importance of events—historians engage in constructive interpretation. And herein lies both a danger to understanding and a great help to understanding. It is dangerous to confuse interpretation with "fact" or with "truth," but it is also necessary to the larger, suprahistorical task of corporate and individual self-interpretation that the interpretive exercise be undertaken.

Thus the first great historian of the church, Eusebius of Caesarea, can hardly be faulted for interpreting the history of the church theologically, in the light both of God's biblical promises and of his own situation, in addition to preserving materials and data from the past history of the church. Eusebius had, after all, lived through the last great persecutions under the emperors Galerius and Maximin Daza; he had seen the rise of young Constantine, the coming of toleration, and the Constantinian patronage of the church; and he had participated in the almost unbelievable event of three hundred bishops meeting safely in one place, under imperial auspices, to debate the future of Christian doctrine. He had participated, he believed, in the dawning of the great age of the church: he could chart a history, in which the church, the body of Christ continuing the work of the Incarnation in this world, had prevailed against the gates of hell and had reached what seemed to be an eschatological vindication after a great tribulation. His history marks the central place of the church in the divinely guaranteed march of history toward the eschaton.

Eusebius' view of history made conceptually possible the Augustinian interpretation of the course of the entirety of world history from the creation onward. Augustine saw the church as the City of God seeking its foundations, with its Lord, outside of the gate of the earthly city, in the heavenly Jerusalem. Just as Eusebius' view of history provided Christians in the fourth and fifth centuries with a sense of the meaning of their place in the community of faith, so did Augustine's view provide Christians throughout the Middle Ages with a sense of their purpose and destiny. Among other things, it was Augustine's picture of the church "in via, on its way toward its heavenly and redemptive goal, that gave the writers of the Middle Ages a sense of the purpose of theology itself and gave, also, the common life of the Middle Ages its pilgrim character, from the practice of pilgrimage to shrines to the creation of the great mendicant orders.

The Reformation, too, brought with it a sense of history. Building upon the late medieval sense of newness or "modernity" and the Renaissance sense of a new grasp of insight by a renewed recourse to the classical and biblical sources of knowledge, the Reformation identified itself as the retrieved and repristinated church after centuries of Babylonian captivity. At the same time, the historians of the Reformation, like the famous Flacius Illyricus, the guiding force of the great project known as the Magdeburg Centuries, who wrote of the "forerunners" of the Reformation, saw the need of stressing the catholicity of the Reformers and the theological rootage of the Reformation in the heritage of Christian truth preserved by the church in all ages. Protestants, ever since, have expressed both a distaste for and a fascination with things medieval as well as a great and positive interest in the theology of the fathers of the first five centuries, before the reputed fall of the church into medieval darkness.

Quite in contrast to these corporately and individually significant but also incredibly theologically biased interpretations and assessments of the history of the church, the study of the church and its teachings also draws on the standard, critical methodology of the historical disciplines. On a very basic level, critical methodology enables us to see that Eusebius had not entered the eschaton and that the success of Christianity in the empire had social and cultural causes. It enables us to see that the institutional church is somewhat less of an image of the "city of God" than some of the medieval writers suggested, while at the same time the Middle Ages cannot be dismissed as a dark, Babylonian Captivity, or the Reformation construed as a radical break with the medieval past. Historical study, from the vantage point of its critical methodology, examines and interprets not only discrete pieces of data but also the broader course of historical events and the theories previously used to make those events meaningful. Thus today Protestants can learn the value of the medieval heritage to Protestantism and its theology without losing sight of the importance of the Reformation.

Church history and the history of doctrine today maintain some of the basic periodizations handed down by the old theological histories, although, of course, recognizing problems with these periodizations in particular and with the division of an essentially seamless history into periods in general. The needs of both academic specialization and cohesive and coherent understanding have led to the division of the historical examination of the church into patristic, medieval, Reformation and post-Reformation, and modern history. Some historians make a stronger distinction between the Reformation and post-Reformation eras, and others speak of a postmodern era in which we presently live. Even if the lines between these periods cannot be rigidly drawn, there are identifiable characteristics of, for example, patristic theology that are not duplicated in the other periods of the history of the church. The Reformation did bring about major changes in the life of the church, indeed, in the whole of Western culture, that still have their impact on us today. And the perspectives on God, man, and the world that dominated the West through the Middle Ages and the Reformation and post-Reformation eras were altered profoundly in the Enlightenment of the eighteenth century, marking the dawn of the "modern" era.

Understanding both the flow of this history and the different characteristics of and issues raised by each of these great periods (not to mention the further subdivision of the periods themselves into shorter segments, each with its own distinctive historical patterns) serves as a guide in interpreting the ideas, cultural monuments, social structures, and institutional developments of our history, many of which continue to have an impact on us. Inasmuch as all ideas and institutions take their form from the culture or society in which they arise—and inasmuch as cultural monuments and social structures frequently outlast the age of their formation and sometimes live on without obvious explanation or warrant into subsequent eras—

knowledge of origins and development is crucial to the critical examination of the cultural and doctrinal patterns of the present.

Beyond this mutual interrelationship and enlightenment of the two subdisciplines, there are larger objective and subjective theological reasons for the study of church history and history of doctrine. Objectively the history of the church and its teachings provides crucial clarification of our present situation in relation both to the biblical foundations of Christianity and to the practices and teachings of the present day. It is certainly a truism, but equally certainly a truism worth repeating, that we cannot understand the present apart from a clear vision of its rootage in the past. The church today, for example, manifests a wide variety of divergent and even conflicting forms of governance: some denominations are governed by bishops who oversee the life of many congregations gathered into a diocese; other denominations identify the minister of each congregation as bishop and presbyter and see to the governance of the whole church through the deliberative work of gatherings of presbyters or presbyteries; and other groups still refuse the notion of denominational oversight, adopting a purely congregational form of government.

When these differences are argued on exegetical grounds alone—and here I realize I will be offending someone—the arguments fall short of cogency. They fail to convince. There are several reasons for this. On the one hand there seem to be at least two church orders in the New Testament—a more "charismatic" order in Paul's congregational epistles (cf. 1 Cor. 12:27ff.) and a more "institutional" order in the Pastoral Epistles. In addition, it is not entirely clear whether or not an "order" for church governance is being suggested in either place. What is clear is that virtually all of the present-day orders of church governance take the names for the various church officers from the New Testament and construct an order out of those names. On the other hand, the history of the church not only manifests the growth and development of several different forms of church governance (particularly in the modern period), it also manifests the social, cultural, and contextual reasons why one order thrives in a given situation and not in another and why certain orders have arisen at particular times. The democratic representative structure of Presbyterianism owes at least as much to the politics of the Swiss cantons as it does to New Testament exegesis. The quasi-episcopal supervisory model found in Lutheranism arose out of the political conditions of sixteenth- and seventeenth-century Germany. Both models can be guided by Scripture, but neither can be explained apart from the history of the church.

The history of the church, therefore, provides a foundation for understanding the forms of church government and the way in which nominally scriptural patterns have been used by Christians throughout the centuries to inform their church governance. This history also offers a salutary lesson in the problems of applying New Testament order to social situations that are radically different from that of the New Testament church. It also shows why, after centuries of meditation on such questions, many church bodies have been willing to place such issues as church governance into the category of adiaphora, "things indifferent," that are not specifically ordained in and by Scripture.

Doctrinal examples of the importance of history to the understanding of issues can be given equally easily. One example will suffice. The orthodox Protestant doctrine of penal substitutionary atonement is firmly rooted in Scripture. That cannot be denied. But it is very difficult to argue purely on the basis of the text of Scripture, without examination of centuries of churchly meditation on Christ's saving work, why this particular formulation, rather than some other, equally biblical statement, has become the doctrinal or systematic centerpiece of orthodox Protestant teaching on the work of Christ. There is biblical language about Christ's work as a ransom from bondage to the powers of the world and ample collateral warrant for such a view in the Pauline contrast of flesh and spirit. There is also biblical language regarding the free gift of reconciling love through the loving example of Christ. The question is not, "Why penal substitutionary atonement?" Scripture clearly speaks of Christ standing in our place as a substitute and bearing for us the divine punishment for sin. The question is, rather, "Why this doctrine as our primary doctrinal position?"

The answer to this latter question is not at all a simple one, and if it is exegetical, it is exegetical in the sense of a churchly exegesis of a whole series of interrelated doctrinal issues over the course of centuries. The early church did not select any particular view of the atonement as primary, but tended to use all of the biblical statements concerning the meaning of Christ's death with equal authority. There was, in short, no systematizing effort made by the early church on the doctrine of Christ's work, no codification of a dogma on this issue. Only in the late twelfth century, in the work of Anselm of Canterbury do we find a concerted attempt to show the logic of the doctrine of the atonement and why the payment made in sacrifice of Christ must be a payment to God rather than to the Devil. In Anselm's *Cur Deus Homo (Why the God-man?)*, then, the satisfaction theory comes to the fore. After several centuries of debate and massive critique and modification at the hands of Aquinas, Scotus, and others, the satisfaction theory passed into the hands of the Reformers. Calvin in particular was responsible for giving it a central place, for couching the language of satisfaction in substitutionary terms, and for replacing the Anselmic notions of satisfaction made to the wronged honor of God with concept of the satisfaction of divine justice.[28]

In the following century, in the theological works of the Protestant orthodox, the doctrine of penal substitutionary atonement reached its final form. An examination of the Protestant orthodox systems, particularly of the way in which they follow the systematic pattern established by Calvin and others of moving from the work of Christ not to the sacraments as the medieval systems did but instead to the application of Christ's work through faith in justification by grace alone, makes clear the fundamental reason for the dominance of penal substitutionary atonement as the basic explanation of Christ's

[28]Cf. Reinhold Seeberg, *Text-book of the History of Doctrines*, trans. Charles Hay, 2 vols. (repr. Grand Rapids: Baker, 1983), 2:68–74, 110–13, 156–58, 399–400.

work. Not only does the doctrine have powerful exegetical warrant on its own terms but, in addition, its view of Christ's work as the acceptance by the sinless Christ of the punishment of our sins revealed the objective ground of a salvation offered apart from human works of satisfaction. It is, in other words, the perfect corollary of the doctrine of justification through faith alone. The doctrine of penal substitutionary atonement comes to the fore in the light of the larger exegetical and systematizing work of the Reformers and their successors.

The objective use and importance of history that we have just now illustrated from church polity and church doctrine point directly to their subjective importance. How is a person to be trained as a Christian in the present? How is the study of theology to provide not merely an objective body of data but also a subjective character, a Christian mind and spirituality? The answers to these questions are certainly not provided in the increasingly secular, non-Christian cultural context of the church in America. Instead, the answers to these questions arise in the context of the self-understanding of the Christian community itself, particularly insofar as that communal self-understanding becomes the basis for individual self-understanding. The study of the history of the church and its teachings is not only an objective, external discipline, it is also a subjective, internal exercise by which and through which the life and mind of the church become an integral part of the life and mind of the individual Christian.

Study of the history of the church and its teaching serves to identify for the individual Christian his or her place in relation to the life and teaching of the church in the present. Some years ago, the television mini-series "Roots" made a great impression on the American public—in fact it assured, among other things, the future of television mini-series! The reason it made such a great impression is that the story itself, like the historical novel on which it was based, charted the quest of one individual, a black American, for his own personal identity. That identity was not given to him either fully or positively by a society that has long oppressed its black members and that, as one of the forms of its oppression, has tended to obscure and to exclude from the societal and cultural history the past of black Americans. Alex Haley's personal quest was a quest for meaning, for identity, for the solidification of his positive place in the present-day life of America in and through the affirmation of his heritage.

The parallel between Alex Haley's search for his roots and the personal, subjective, and spiritual appropriation of church history ought to be clear. There is no overt oppression of Christians in this culture, and in this country we never had to struggle to gain recognition of the importance and rightful place of Christianity in our culture. We did, of course, need to guarantee the freedom of expression of various forms of religion—but that is another issue. Christians in America are not overtly oppressed simply because they are Christian. Nonetheless, as our society and its values grow less and less Christian and therefore less and less supportive of and even hospitable to the Christian way of life and belief, our identity as Christians and the Christian heritage of our past became obscured. Only by engagement in a quest for our Christian "roots" can this heritage be known, its cultural values understood and maintained, and our own personal identity as Christians in Christian community be affirmed and perpetuated. Recognition of this personal, existential need for roots is hardly new: it was Cicero who said, "Not to know the events that happened before one was born is to remain always a child"; and the identity of the children of Israel was passed on from generation to generation in the confessional recitation of the history of the people, "My father was a wandering Aramean . . ." (Deut. 26:5ff.).

THE UNITY OF BIBLICAL AND HISTORICAL STUDIES

Biblical and church historical studies are closely related to each other and ought to be studied with a consistent recognition of their interdependence. A historical, developmental perspective presents us with an essentially seamless flow of events from the era of the Old Testament, through the so-called intertestamental period and the era of earliest Christianity in the New Testament, on into the patristic, medieval, Reformation, post-Reformation, and modern eras. Not only can we speak of a continuous development or trajectory of Judeo-Christian religion, we can also speak of a continuous cultural and social development around and with the Judeo-Christian trajectory that places it into the ongoing history of civilization and of religions. Separation of the canon of Scripture from the culture and the history around it is thus doctrinally justifiable but interpretatively problematic. The culture of the ancient Near East and of the Roman world must be brought to bear on the interpretation of Scripture.

Far from creating a problem for church and theology, these historical continuities point toward a continuity in the development of the Christian community and its message that not only informs the study of theology but, in a profound and fundamental way, makes that study possible. The biblical message is not a message from the past that sits, as a self-contained and isolated canon, on a bookshelf waiting for the proper moment to speak and then, having spoken, returning to its shelf until such time as it may again prove useful. If that were the case, the Bible would be a normative reference book, comparable in function to the *Encyclopedia Britannica* or *Webster's Unabridged Dictionary*. Instead, the biblical message is and has always been a message situated in the present life of the religious community, a message heard as normative in the context of other messages, some based on it and some not, each with its own degree of authority and usefulness. The ongoing life of the religious community—the history of the church—modeled in faith and in practice upon an interpretation of the biblical message in relation to the social and cultural situation of the times, carries forward the message, not as a dead letter but as a living Word into our present.

From a methodological point of view the disciplines also form a basic unity. The same, essentially historical, textual, grammatical, contextual, and critical method is used by Bible scholars, church historians, historians of doctrine, and secular historians. This is not to deny the fact that Bible scholars and

historians of church and doctrine frequently hold theological
presuppositions concerning the truth of the message contained
in the documents they analyze, presuppositions of a somewhat
different order than a secular historian's presumption of the
truthful intention of the sources he analyzes. The point needs to
be made, nonetheless, that the basic methods of analysis are the
same and that the basic rules of hermeneutics observed are
identical. Historical method is historical method. Differences in
method concerning the presence or absence of a distinction
between "fact" and "interpretation" or concerning the kind of
"meaning" to be found in history (i.e., moral conclusions, self-
understanding, and so forth) are shared alike by historical
investigators of Scripture, church, and the Second World War.
The issue is one of the competence of method and the potential
scope of its conclusions. In any case, one methodology, replete
as it is with its own internal disputes, is used by biblical
scholars, by historians of church and doctrine, and by secular
historians.

A concrete indication of this unity of perspective and
method is seen in that the works on "earliest Christianity,"
whether on the general history of the New Testament church
and its mission or on the theology of the New Testament, at the
same time that they respect the canon of the New Testament in
theological terms, tend to argue the meaning of the New
Testament in terms of its general cultural context, its roots in
the Old Testament and the intertestamental literature, and,
quite strikingly, its implications as seen in the writing of the
apostolic fathers of the early second century. Ignatius' language
concerning the Incarnation illuminates discussion of the purpose
of the infancy narratives in the gospels. The docetistic attempt
to rationalize away the problem of Christ's humanity and to
remove the difficulty of teaching the union of the divine with a
finite and fleshly body by denying the reality of Christ's
humanity is countered directly by Ignatius with reference to the
Davidic lineage and human birth of Jesus. If indeed the priority
of Mark and the later addition of the infancy narratives to the
gospel accounts are accepted on the basis of historical and

textual analysis, the arguments presented by Ignatius point toward the theological significance of the addition.

The early church, beginning in the first century during the time of the preparation of our canonical New Testament, not only saw the danger to Christian teaching of a failure to deal with the true humanity of Jesus of Nazareth, it also moved toward a doctrinal solution to that problem by concentrating on the question of the divine and human identity of Jesus. In this sense, the infancy narratives, like the prologue to the gospel of John, taken together with the arguments of Ignatius and, after him, the second-century apologists, lie on a doctrinal trajectory that leads to the consideration of the "person" of Christ in the third, fourth, and fifth centuries. The development of the language of one person of Christ in two natures by Tertullian and other writers of the early church can be understood, valued, and used by us only if we recognize what it attempted to say about the apostolic witness to Christ.

Another instance of early patristic testimony adding a new dimension to the interpretation of the biblical materials is the statement found in 1 Clement concerning the ministry of the apostle Paul. Clement testifies to seven imprisonments of Paul and to Paul's mission to the "whole world" as far as "the limit of the West."[29] In the light of Paul's stated desire to journey to Spain after his ministry in Rome (Rom. 15:28) and the rather buoyant conclusion of Acts (28:30–31) Clement's early testimony (ca. A.D. 100) to a mission to Spain and the way in which it opens up the Pauline chronology ought to be taken seriously. At the very least, historical study must inquire carefully whether or not Clement's words are merely an elaboration of Romans 15:28 or a glimpse into a history otherwise lost to us.

In addition to these and many other instances of the interpretative relationships that exist between the writings of the canonical New Testament and the documents of the early church, the continuity between the one body of literature and the other must be recognized in the shape and contents of the canon of the New Testament itself. In A.D. 117 the terminus ad

---

[29]1 Clement, 5, in ANF, 1:6.

quem of the episcopate of Ignatius of Antioch, the canon of the
New Testament had not yet been defined by the church. The
strict identification of the canon of the New Testament took
place over the next two centuries as Christian communities
around the Mediterranean basin shared the apostolic writings
over against writings that claimed to be apostolic but contained
doctrines unacceptable to the faith of the church. Thus, between
the beginning of the second and the beginning of the fourth
century, the gospel of Mark, a document probably of Roman
origin; the gospel of Matthew, a document probably of Syrian
provenance; the epistles of Paul to the Corinthians, which were
originally in possession of the Corinthian church, and so forth,
became the common property of Christians everywhere.
During the same period, the heretical Marcion proposed a
purified canon of exclusively Pauline materials plus the gospel
of Luke, purged of references to the Old Testament, and the
Gnostics offered a wide variety of gospels and epistles written
under the names of the apostles.

Inasmuch as the apostles themselves had not created a
canonical witness to Christ limited to their own literary
productions, the church of the second and third centuries was
pressed to perform the task itself. Since, moreover, many
theologically unacceptable writings were put forth under the
names of the apostles—like the Gospel and Acts of Thomas—
and since several theologically important documents were
known to have been written not by the apostles themselves but
by followers of the apostles—like the Gospel of Mark and
Luke-Acts—the church needed to identify a standard of
canonicity in some sense external to the books themselves yet
firmly grounded in the apostolic preaching itself. In the so-
called Rule of Faith found in slightly different forms in the
writings of Irenaeus, Hippolytus, and Tertullian, the church
found that standard. The Rule of Faith was a distillate of the
apostolic preaching very much like the Apostle's Creed in form
and content. As R. B. Rackham argued, all of the articles of the
Rule can be identified in the apostolic preaching of the Book of

Acts.[30] In addition, confession of the Rule excluded both the Gnostic distinction between the good high God and the deficient creator and the Gnostic denial of the reality of Christ's bodily existence and death; applied to purportedly apostolic documents, the rule excluded those of a Gnostic and Marcionite theology. This canonical principle, together with the assumption of apostolic authorship or close proximity to direct apostolic witness, made possible the creation of the canon.

Granting this historical and churchly creation of the canon itself, it becomes impossible to sever New Testament study from the study of the history of the church and its doctrines. The identification of the New Testament belongs to the history of the church, and therefore in a very real sense the study of church history contains the completion of the historical study of the New Testament. The Protestant *sola Scriptura* is, therefore, as much a mandate to the study of the history of the church as is the Roman Catholic emphasis on tradition. In fact, Protestant theology in general needs to be more conscious, in a functional and constructive sense, of the importance of the tradition in mediating both Scripture and fundamental understanding of Scripture to the present. Thus, Pannenberg has recently argued:

> Church history is not just a particular discipline, as biblical theology can be said to be. It embraces the whole of theology, whereas biblical theology as a discipline can only *per nefas* [lit., going beyond proper jurisdiction], and the individual exegete only by exercising considerable courage, transcend the limits of their own discipline in order to consider its contribution to theology as a whole. The matter cannot be the concern uniquely of historical-critical biblical science. In contrast it is the field of church history as church history which stretches beyond its formal boundaries into biblical theology on the one side and dogmatics and practical theology on the other.[31]

Pannenberg's comments are echoed, moreover, in Ebeling's citation of the maxim that church history can be understood "as

---

[30]Richard B. Rackham, *The Acts of the Apostles: An Exposition* (London: Methuen, 1901; 14th ed. 1951), pp. lxix–lxxi.

[31]Pannenberg, *Theology and the Philosophy of Science*, p. 392.

a history of the exegesis of the New Testament Scripture" and by Schaff's statement that

> Church History is the connecting link between Exegetical and Systematic theology. It embraces all that is of permanent interest in the past fortunes of Christendom. But in a wider sense it covers also the whole extent of exegesis and runs parallel with it. . . . [Church history] is by far the most extensive and copious part of sacred learning, and supplies material to all other departments. If exegesis is the root, church history is the main trunk. We are connected with the Bible through the intervening links of the past and all its educational influences, and cannot safely disregard the wisdom and experience of ages.[32]

The statement that "church history is the history of exegesis" contains only some hyperbole: it is more accurate, strictly speaking, to say with Schaff that church history "covers" or contains "the whole of exegesis." And, beyond Schaff, we must recognize that church history not only "supplies materials" but also provides a heuristic key to unlocking their meaning. The study of history not only presents us with the doctrinal, ethical, and practical or ministerial materials of past generations of Christians, it also presents us with the context for understanding why those materials appear in their particular forms and with their own specific ways of expressing and addressing issues. All of these considerations point us toward the conclusion that the study of history is both a hermeneutical and a spiritually formative task.

More important than any number of examples we can offer is the cultivation of an approach to historical study that is fundamentally exegetical and interpretive, that continues into these other areas of study the hermeneutical emphasis necessary to the study of Scripture. The history of Christian doctrine, in other words, ought not to be reduced to a list of formulae to be memorized for the sake of avoiding heresy. The issue in studying the formulae is to understand their interpretive relationship to the Christian message and the way in which they

---

[32]Schaff, *Theological Propaedeutic*, pp. 234–35; cf. Ebeling, *The Study of Theology*, p. 77.

have served in particular historical contexts to convey that message and, in addition, to preserve it into the future. Historical formulations, such as the Nicene doctrine of the Trinity and the Chalcedonian doctrine of the person of Christ, become elements of our doctrinal perspective today, not as contemporary results of New Testament exegesis, but as interpretive tools marking out the history of the ongoing significance of the gospel—on its way to becoming the gospel for us.

COMPARATIVE RELIGION AND HISTORY OF RELIGIONS

I have already, at several points, indicated the importance of a larger cultural, historical, religious, and intellectual context to the understanding of the documents in the Bible and in the history of the church and to the theological task in the present. This larger context is surveyed and interpreted through the study of comparative religion and the history of religions. Christian theologians and the organizers of seminary curricula have been slow to acknowledge the importance of these subjects to the study of theology and, as noted in my analysis of Pannenberg, have thereby become responsible at least in part for the unproductive severance between the university study of religion and the seminary study of theology typical of American academia. They have also become responsible for an isolation of theology from the world around it and, as a result, for the frequently felt inability of contemporary theology to address the world and the culture in terms that actually speak to the contemporary situation.

There are several reasons for this separation of the study of comparative religion and history of religions from the traditional study of theology, none of them negligible. In the first place, there is the issue of the necessary particularity of a religion and its message of salvation. From a religious and theological point of view, whereas value is the necessary presupposition of the churchly study of Christianity, there is no value in the generalized study of religion. Christians, Jews, and

Muslims can, at very least, agree that religion in general is not what delivers human beings from the spiritual problems of life in this world. What delivers human beings from the spiritual problems of life in this world is a particular religion with a particular message of salvation. If we set aside our particularity, we set aside the very thing that makes possible our message of salvation. From the purely religious viewpoint of the Christian community, the study of contemporary Judaism, Islam, Buddhism, Hinduism, or Taoism is not useful to the salvation of individuals. As Cyprian of Carthage said in the third century A.D.: "Outside of the church, there is no salvation." Why study religions comparatively when we understand salvation in a strictly Christian sense?

In the second place, courses in comparative religion and history of religions have tended to relativize religion and set aside precisely what particular religions value the most: their particularity. The study of religion in general has tended to seek out broad themes, large-scale mythic constructions—such as teachings of heavenly redeemers and life beyond death—and to point toward common human aspirations and hopes underlying all religion. The effect of this investigation, whether intended or not, has been in many cases to evacuate these generalized symbols of salvation and eternal reality of genuine meaning and, in the name of objectivity, to sever the language and claims of religion from the real world of daily human existence.

Third, Christian theology and the history of religions method have a history of negative interaction: one need only mention Richard Reitzenstein's work *The Hellenistic Mystery Religions* and Wilhelm Bousset's *Kyrios Christos* to make the point. Reitzenstein examined, among other features of the Hellenistic mystery religions, their emphasis on myths of a dying and rising god, while Bousset concentrated on the transplanting of Christianity from its original Palestinian and Jewish context into "the soil of Hellenistic mysticism." The result, in both cases, was a placement of Christianity into a broad, ancient history of religions and, from the point of view of Christian theology, a rather disconcerting association of the main teachings of the church concerning the divinity and the resurrection of Christ with Hellenistic religion rather than with Judaism or with the teachings of Jesus.

All of these factors have contributed to the separation of Christian theology from the study of comparative religion and the history of religions. Nonetheless, the separation has not been total and the relationship, when pursued, not entirely negative. Indeed, the use of history of religions and the comparative study of religions in biblical studies has generally proved very fruitful and, as I will try to argue, ought to prove as fruitful in the study of theology. There can be no doubt that the historical study of ancient Egyptian, Mesopotamian, and Canaanite religion has proved highly significant to the understanding of the development of Israelite monotheism, of the way in which Israel saw the working of God in history, and of the confrontation between the Yahwism of the prophets and the Baalism of the Canaanites, and of those Israelites swayed by the agrarian culture and religion of the Promised Land.

Despite the uproar once caused by Reitzenstein and Bousset, history of religions and the comparative study of religions can also prove useful to our theological understanding of the New Testament and of the early church, particularly in view of the success of Christianity in moving from a Palestinian, Jewish context to a broader Mediterranean, Graeco-Roman context. The success of this cross-cultural transmission of Christianity offers a way of assessing the religious and theological significance of Christianity over against its religious competitors: it is not a useful explanation of the success of Christianity simply to claim that it is true. Truth is not, after all, always appealing to the human mind and heart. It is useful, however, both historically and theologically to see that Christianity, with its teaching about death and resurrection, was religiously understandable to a population schooled in the similar beliefs of the mystery religions, but that Christianity added a historical focus on Jesus of Nazareth, a high ethical content, and a philosophically significant monotheism to the message of death and resurrection, issues and themes that the mysteries could not match. Christianity gave to the culture something that it desired deeply: it answered the ethical, religious, and philosophical questionings of the Graeco-Roman culture. We learn this not so much by reading the New Testament and the writings of the fathers but by comparing those churchly texts with the religious and philosophical movements of the first and second centuries.

Christianity also gained from the culture an ability to address religious and ethical problems on a high philosophical plane—something that it had not received directly from Judaism. There was, of course, the precedent of the Platonic theology of Philo of Alexandria, but this was hardly a model accepted generally by the Judaism of the time or, for that matter, by the disciples of Jesus. When, however, the early church moved definitively across the cultural divide into the Hellenistic world, it rapidly recognized the ability of the Christian message to supercede the popular religion of the day and to address the higher ethical questions and the monotheistic tendencies of Graeco-Roman philosophy. By recognizing the elements of truth known to these philosophies and by acknowledging the one divine source of truth, the early church was able to discern in Graeco-Roman philosophy and ethics an old covenant given to the Gentiles vaguer and less revelatory of divine truth but nonetheless parallel to the old covenant given to the Jews. This theological understanding of Gentile tradition allowed the early church to draw on the great philosophies and create a Christian amalgam that was, in Paul's words, "neither Jew nor Greek," but that drew on the best of both traditions and set aside what was unusable in both.

In fact, it is the historical and comparative study of religion that makes possible an understanding of the character and the success of the cross-cultural transmission of Christianity throughout its history. Although some recent writers have tended to view Christianity as a "Western" and even monocultural phenomenon apart from its recent extension into the Third World, this is far from being a historically accurate approach to the Christian faith. Historically, Christianity represents an initially Palestinian, Jewish religious movement, introduced first into a Hellenistic Greek context, next into a Latin cultural and linguistic context and then into various Celtic, Germanic, and Slavic contexts. There has hardly been an era in the history of the church in which the gospel and the attendant doctrines of the believing community have not been addressed to a new cultural and religious context—and, therefore, explained in terms understandable to cultural and (non-Christian) religious groups very different in their language and worldview from the earliest Christians. Just as historical and comparative study of religion is essential to our understanding of the biblical message, so also is it crucial to our understanding of the historical message of the church.

As an antidote to the tendency of many contemporary "theologians" of comparative religion or religion in general to find the lowest or most banal common denominator as the ground for a synthesis of world religions, traditional, conservative Christianity needs to listen to the words of Ernest Troeltsch about the place of Christianity among the world religions and about the importance of history of religions to the method of theology. There is a need to guide our study between the extremes of a generalized religiosity that follows no religion and a Barthian rejection of religion on the claim that Christianity is something else. Christianity is a religion that claims ultimacy for itself in a world of religions. Troeltsch could argue, on the basis of perspectives drawn from history of religions methodology, that

> what is to be expected from the few great breakthroughs of the religious principle . . . is not the aimless vagary of a multiplicity of revelations but the victory of the purest and most profound idea of God. As the history of religions shows, this idea of God is not to be sought in some kind of scientistic religion or in a general principle of religion that abstracts only what the various religions hold in common and for that reason overlooks their important differences. It is to be sought, rather, among the positive, historical, religious orientations and revelations.[33]

Nor did Troeltsch accept the argument that historical method demands the kind of neutrality that bars the way to a

---

[33]Ernst Troeltsch, *The Absoluteness of Christianity*, trans. David Reid (Richmond: John Knox, 1971), p. 103.

declaration of the superiority of the Christian faith. "History," according to Troeltsch, "is the sphere of knowledge because it is the sphere of the individual and nonrecurrent" with which, nonetheless, is found "something universally valid—or something connected with the universally valid."[34] Within the relative and conditioned we see an "indication of the unconditional." This coincidence or intersection of the relative and the absolute, the particular and the universal, not only permits Troeltsch to argue the existence of higher religions, it also provides him with a religious index, within history, of the achievement of Christianity, with an indication that, on historical grounds, Christianity offers "the highest religious truth that has relevance to us."[35] Christianity is, arguably, "the strongest and most concentrated revelation of personalistic religious apprehension." It alone among the higher religions "takes empirical reality as actually given and experienced, builds upon it, transforms it, and at length raises it up to a new level."[36]

Thus the study of the history of religions and of comparative religion belongs to theological study and to theological formulation inasmuch as it provides us with a sense of the larger world context within which Christianity exists and from which Christianity must learn issues and problems that it must address. Such a study, however, must not cause a relativization of the Christian message or a loss of its particularity. From its very beginnings, the Judeo-Christian tradition encountered and responded to its religious context in the larger world—first Canaanite, Egyptian, and Mesopotamian and later Greek and Roman religion. Our understanding of this tradition rests in no small measure on our theological assessment of these encounters. We saw this point illustrated in our brief discussion of the Old Testament and the broadening of Israelite monotheism during the exilic period. Similar examples appear in the discussions of the New Testament and of church history.

---

[34]Ibid., p. 106.
[35]Ibid., pp. 106–7.
[36]Ibid., p. 112.

When we extend this model to contemporary theological understanding, it becomes apparent that Christianity stands today in much the same relation to the great religions of the world—Buddhism, Hinduism, Taoism, and so forth—as it once stood to the religions of the ancient Mediterranean world. Not only must we understand these religions in order to grasp the very real impact they have had and are having on segments of our own culture and society, but we must also understand them in order that a Christian theology can address the world around it in a cogent and convincing way. And, if our past is any index to our present, we may engage in this part of our study in the hope that our Christianity will be strengthened and our Christian message both broadened and made more relevant to the needs of our world.

3

THE THEOLOGICAL DISCIPLINES: CONTEMPORARY STATEMENT AND PRACTICE

The historical sweep of the Judeo-Christian tradition, from the call of Abraham to the present-day expression of faith in God, has always had a doctrinal and a practical dimension. What has become, in our study and practice of theology, a disciplinary division into systematic and practical fields has always existed in some form and exists today for the church whether one looks at a seminary curriculum or at a pastor's weekly work. The study of theology, as it moves through its biblical and historical roots toward the expression of present-day concerns, ought to find itself immersed in profound questions concerning the impact of the biblical and historical materials on the ways in which people think and act. The division between "systematic" and "practical" is nothing more or less than a statement that the life of the Christian community can be distinguished into categories of faith and obedience, of what is believed and what is done. It should also be clear that this distinction of aspects of the religious life or of elements of a theological curriculum does not permit a radical separation of fields of study or aspects of church practice: what is believed not only ought to relate to what is done, it ought also to govern and guide it; what is done or, better, what is learned from what has been done, ought, likewise, to draw consistently on and, occasionally, modify the expression of belief, though not the substance. Thus the study of the historical disciplines—of the biblical and the churchly materials—offers a foundation for the formation and encouragement of individuals, for the development of intellectual, spiritual, and moral character.

Since the systematic and the practical disciplines are really no more than the formalization, for the purpose of study and analysis, of the church's beliefs and practices, grown naturally out of and built on the historical experience of the Christian community, their existence does not at all depend on seminary study or on the creation of a particular kind of theological encyclopedia during the nineteenth century. In other words, "systematic" and "practical" theology are the formal expressions, in an academic context, of the faith and obedience that have always been a part of the life of the believing community. In our own time, the formal elements of these disciplines—including a maze of subdisciplines—have tended to obscure the fact that systematic and practical theology are nothing more than the studied presentation of what the church believes and how the church lives and behaves. In the following discussion, granting the historical rootage of these two major divisions of theological study, we will attempt to outline an approach to systematics and to praxis—or, as the title of the chapter indicates, to contemporary statement and contemporary practice.

Systematic theology is a much used and a much abused term, but it remains the broadest usage for the contemporary task of gathering together the elements of our faith into a coherent whole. In making this statement, I have already, in a sense, defined the field and a fundamental approach to it. Just as the entirety of biblical and church historical study can be gathered under the larger methodological rubric of "historical theology," so can all of the contemporizing, constructive disciplines be gathered together under the rubric of "systematic theology." This broad usage is not always observed, and "systematic theology" is frequently taken to be a synonym for "dogmatics" or "doctrinal theology"—but it is both arguable and highly instructive to focus on the broad usage as part of the methodological question of the unity of theological study and as, in fact, the proper meaning of the term.

Whereas "dogmatic" or "doctrinal theology" necessarily indicates a restrictive focus on the examination and exposition of the dogmas of the church—of the doctrines of the Trinity and the person of Christ, of human nature, sin and grace, of the church and the last things, the standard *loci* of classical dogmatics—"systematic theology" implies a discussion of those and of other topics that moves beyond exposition of churchly doctrine to philosophical questioning, presuppositional statement, argumentative defense, and cohesive analysis in the present context. It is very clear, for example, that Barth entitled his theology *Church Dogmatics* for the purpose of excluding from the outset of discussion all reference to philosophical categories and apologetic interests. And although his dogmatics has a certain cohesion when considered on its own terms and with a view to its own internal logic, it has very little reference to or application in the present context.[1] Gerhard Ebeling well says:

> While [dogmatics] is used in a limited way of the coherent presentation of religious doctrine, thus predominantly being set off against ethics . . . the expression "systematic theology" has the tendency to embrace everything in theology methodologically oriented to the question of contemporary validity and to the testing of the claim to truth.[2]

To make the point in another way: just as the ethical life of Christians must be lived in the world and in a particular social context that is not "Christian" but that, nonetheless, shares certain beliefs and practices with the Christian community, so also does the intellectual and spiritual life of Christians take place in a larger social context. Systematic theology must be "oriented to the question of contemporary validity" and must consider philosophical and apologetic issues if only because the believing community cannot exist for long in dialogue only

---

[1] Cf. the pointed critique in Heinz Zahrnt, *The Question of God*, trans R. A. Wilson (London: Collins, 1969), p. 117.

[2] Gerhard Ebeling, *The Study of Theology*, trans. Duane Priebe (Philadelphia: Fortress, 1978), p. 126.

with itself and in ignorance of the issues being addressed or demanding to be addressed in the world around it.

Once it is recognized that systematic theology, simply by being genuinely "systematic," must ask the larger question of coherence in the contemporary context, the concept of a "systematic theology" can become the second focus of our discussion of the unity of theological discourse. Just as the history of doctrine is a unifying discipline that must be responsive to the entire trajectory of the Judeo-Christian tradition in its cultural and historical context and to the way in which that trajectory points toward the present, so also is systematic theology a unitive discipline that must be responsive to the findings and claims of the other theological disciplines: the historical model seeks chronological and developmental cohesion while the systematic model seeks constructive, relational, and conceptual cohesion in the present. The very nature of this constructive and cohesive task demands the use of historical and critical, doctrinal or dogmatic, philosophical and apologetic categories. Systematic theology is, then, correctly understood in terms of its methodological comprehension of the whole gamut of contemporizing and constructive disciplines. The attempt to identify systematics with a limited set of these disciplines undermines its proper method and negates its basic task. Pannenberg sums up the task of systematics in terms of the universality of the theological task. Systematic theology, he points out, is concerned with the "faithfulness" both of "theology itself and . . . of the Christian church" to the "revelation of God in Jesus Christ," but precisely because this special focus of theology on Christ leads to speech about God, the theological task must be open to "all truth whatever." The universality of the subject leads to the universal outlook of the task.[3]

Systematic theology, then, must consider all of the constructive topics in theology—dogmatics, apologetics, philosophical theology, philosophy and phenomenology of religion,

---

[3]Wolfhart Pannenberg, *Basic Questions in Theology: Collected Essays*, trans. George H. Kehm, 2 vols. (repr. Philadelphia: Westminster, 1983), 1:1.

ethics—and draw them out in the light of the materials provided in the historical analyses of biblical study and church history. In an academically extended or expanded model such as that proposed by Pannenberg—and we might add, suitable to the constructive discussion of the Christian message in the larger world context of the twentieth century—the "history of religions" and "philosophy of religion," as objective disciplines distinct from apologetics in its missiological application, would also fall under the category of systematics. The constructive as well as the critical impact of social and humane sciences like anthropology, sociology, and psychology would also be felt in systematic theology. Thus part of the systematic task today is the establishment of principles and procedures for the theological use of the results of these disciplines, a task analogous to the discussion, begun in the Middle Ages and still going on in the present, concerning the use of philosophical categories in theology.[4]

DOGMATIC OR DOCTRINAL THEOLOGY

Doctrinal or dogmatic theology, simply defined, is the contemporary exposition of the greater doctrines of the church. The two parts of this definition must be balanced evenly: dogmatics cannot just be the recitation of the doctrinal statements of the church in a topical rather than a historical order nor can it be just the contemporary exposition of someone's theological ideas, no matter how brilliant they might be. The doctrines must be churchly, and the exposition, also churchly in its basic attitude and approach, must be contemporary in its expression. If the contemporary aspect of the definition is lost, the exposition lapses into a reconstructive, historically defined approach that can at best produce for present-day examination a doctrinal overview from a bygone era. This kind of theology is no better than the attempt to take a particular document from a past era—even a document as valuable as Calvin's *Institutes* or

---

[4]Cf. my "Giving Direction to Theology: the Scholastic Dimension," *Journal of the Evangelical Theological Society* 28,2 (June 1985): 183–93.

Aquinas' *Summa Theologiae*—and use it as a textbook in theology. The past must be consulted, but not copied without regard to the new historical and cultural situation in which we find ourselves. If, on the other hand, the great doctrines of the church are not addressed, the exposition lapses into subjectivity and personal or even idiosyncratic statement. The value of such theologies is obviously limited—and limited to a nonchurchly constituency!

There is, therefore, in dogmatic or doctrinal theology a clear relationship between contemporary faith-statement and the normative doctrinal constructs known as dogmas. The question for dogmatic theology is precisely how these dogmas relate to the biblical witness on which they have been founded, to the larger body of doctrines that belongs to theology but that has not been as closely defined as the so-called dogmas, and to the ability of the contemporary theologian or minister to proclaim the significance of the biblical witness for the present. The historical element in the method of systematic theology enters at this point, inasmuch as the reconstruction of the meaning both of Scripture and of churchly dogmas and doctrines is the necessary basis for the identification of their contemporary significance.

Dogmas, then, are not the sole content of dogmatics. Dogmatics presents the whole body of Christian doctrine—but it does so "dogmatically," that is, with a view toward the regulatory character of dogmas and, by extension, with a view toward the regulatory character of the language of doctrine in general. This latter statement demands some explanation. The term *dogma* derives from the Greek *dokein*, to think or believe, and it indicates a fundamental tenet of thought or belief. The derivation is not modern: the word "dogma" appears in classical Greek, indicating either a propositional truth of philosophy or an authoritative decree in law. The early church took over the term and used it as a characterization of divine truths, although virtually always in statements distinguishing between specifically divine or revealed dogmas and human dogmas having no authority in the church. In the Renaissance and Reformation the term was used particularly with reference to human decrees belonging to the church as distinct from the teachings of biblical revelation. This is the sense of the term adopted by Adolf von Harnack in his *History of Dogma*.[5] By way of contrast, largely because of later usage both Catholic and Protestant, dogma has come to indicate the churchly determination of doctrine by ecumenical consensus, specifically the dogmas of the Trinity and the person of Christ. Here, of course, the connotation of the term is positive.

Granting this historical use of the term *dogma*, it is not at all surprising that doctrinal theology was not referred to as "dogmatics" until the seventeenth century and that the use of "dogmatic theology" as a title for the exposition of a body of Christian doctrine did not become common until the eighteenth. In addition, inasmuch as the doctrines that can be identified as ecclesiastical dogmas in the strictest sense are relatively few in number (i.e., Trinity and the person of Christ), the adoption of the term *dogmatics* for doctrinal theology is primarily a reference to the regulative or normative character of the way in which all doctrines are set forth rather than a reference to concentration on particular doctrines. As Ebeling argues, "dogmatic theology" intends to produce assertions of truth—it is an assertoric as opposed to a problematic form of discourse.[6]

This assertive character of dogmatics arises only in the context of the whole of a theological study in which dogmatic declaration is one of the final steps. Doctrinal theology, given its dogmatic character, cannot arise prior to biblical and historical theology and cannot impose itself as a methodological rule on biblical or historical study: it is a result, not a premise of the other disciplines. Nonetheless, this regulatory function does stand in a fundamental relationship to the other primary theological disciplines. In the churchly hermeneutical circle identified previously as moving from the text of Scripture to the tradition that has carried forward the meaning of the text into

---

[5]Adolf von Harnack, *History of Dogma* trans. Neil Buchanan, 7 vols. (New York: Dover, 1961); cf. Ebeling, *The Study of Theology*, pp. 128–29.
[6]Ibid., p. 131.

the present, and as including the exegete, minister, theologian, or student of theology, the dogmatic conclusion marks the closure of the circle. The result of the theological task is a theologically regulative conclusion that not only expresses the faith of the believing community in the present but also returns, via the tradition, to the text and provides a set of theological boundary-concepts for the continuing work of theology.

The mistaken self-exaltation of which doctrinal or dogmatic theology is all too easily capable can, moreover, be described and avoided in terms of this hermeneutical model. If a theologian exalts any particular doctrinal construction and insists that it become the key to interpreting the entirety of Scripture and to organizing the entirety of theological system, the scriptural Word becomes stifled by a human a priori, by what is perhaps a brilliant but nonetheless false contrivance of a particular theological ego. It is an error for a systematic theologian to assume that any particular systematization of a biblical idea or group of biblical ideas can become the basis for the interpretation of texts in which those ideas or doctrines do not appear.

This would appear, on the surface, to be a very simple rule—a rule that no right-minded theologian would violate. When, however, we cite particular examples, the frequency with which the rule has been violated becomes obvious. The so-called predestinarian system advocated by a few, mostly modern, Reformed theologians is one example; the radical Christocentrism (or Christomonism) of several nineteenth-century theologians and of neoorthodoxy is another; the use of justification and reconciliation as central dogmas by Albrecht Ritschl, yet another; and the emphasis on God as love to the exclusion of other attributes, typical of Ritschlianism and of American "Christocentric liberalism," still another.

Each of these "centrisms"—with, presumably, the best of theological intentions—ignores the variety of the biblical witness and the variety of the church's tradition of interpretation and forgets that the unity of the proclamation and the unity of any system of doctrine arises out of the biblical witness rather than being imposed on it. The proper hermeneutical approach within theological system is one that arises out of biblical and historical exegesis—that arises out of exegesis not only via the commentary but also via the disciplines of biblical theology and history of doctrine. Whereas the history of Christian doctrine provides systematic theology with a preliminary collation and interpretation of the biblical materials that precede any contemporary system in time and supply a churchly precedent for theological formulation in the present, biblical theology, insofar as it is a contemporary theological exercise and not an account of its own past, provides a preliminary collation and interpretation of the Scriptures that precede contemporary theological system not temporally but logically, in view of the proper principles and priorities of system itself.

The method and organization of doctrinal theology, its principles and its priorities, rest on two foundations, the biblical and the historical. In the spirit of the Reformation, Protestant theology accepts the canonical Scriptures as its primary norm and the history of the church's faith, particularly as it is expressed in the great ecumenical creeds and the great churchly confessions of the Reformation, as a secondary guide in matters of doctrine and interpretation. In other words, the canon of Scripture functions as a point of division of the larger tradition. As indicated previously, the canon is historically vague but doctrinally precise.

The biblical norm provides doctrinal theology with its primary topics, while the historical norm provides theology with an ongoing meditation on and interpretive elaboration of the contents of Scripture in the light of the historical experience of the believing community. The philosophical materials, both historical and contemporary, will provide critical and collateral standards for formulation—frequently taking the form of checks on the language and reasonability of our formulations. The way in which these materials are appropriated and used in doctrinal theology can and ought to evidence the unity of theological study as a whole and ought to contribute, both theoretically and practically, to the ongoing life of the Christian community.

Biblical theology, as discussed in the preceding chapter, is a theological discipline intended specifically to provide an overview of the religion and theology of the Old Testament and the New Testament in their own historical contexts. As such, it offers systematic theology an interpretive bridge to the overarching meaning of the biblical witness and its many theologies and themes. Inasmuch, moreover, as this interpretive bridge is methodologically and intentionally distinct from the bridge created by the history of doctrine, it serves not only as another point of contact between ourselves and the biblical text but also as a check on our potential exaltation of the tradition, as given by the history of doctrine, over the text. In other words, biblical theology has the potential of reopening the text of Scripture for systematic use on issues and topics where traditional interpretations have either been mistaken or have led to omissions of insights of themes from our theological systems.

By way of example, few systems of doctrinal theology deal with the issue of anthropomorphism and anthropopathism in God-language except to note it as a problem to be overcome on the way to a clear presentation of the doctrine of God. Yet biblical theology, particularly the theology of the Old Testament, helps us to recognize that the description of God with language drawn from the human form and from the human emotions is intrinsic to the biblical message and, in fact, provides the foundation for our identification of God as "personal." In this case, the results of biblical theology demand a reshaping of the systematic theological discussion of the doctrine of God and a fuller use of the category of anthropomorphisms and anthropopathisms in our theology.[7]

Another, perhaps more serious example is the traditional use of the terms "Son of Man" and "Son of God" as a point of reference to the humanity and divinity of Jesus, respectively.

---

[7]Cf. the discussions of anthropomorphisms and anthropopathisms in Gustav Friedrich Oehler, *Old Testament Theology*, trans. George Day (Edinburgh: T. & T. Clark, 1873), pp. 111–12; Hermann Schultz, *Old Testament Theology*, trans. J. A. Paterson, 2d ed., 2 vols. (Edinburgh: T. & T. Clark, 1898), 2:103–11; and Ludwig Köhler, *Theology of the Old Testament*, trans. A. S. Todd (Philadelphia: Westminster, 1957), pp. 22–25.

This usage is not only typical of the early church and of the church of the medieval and Reformation periods, it remains typical of systems of theology (usually—and unfortunately—"conservative" systems) even in our own day.[8] The early church brought the Palestinian, Jewish terminology of Son of Man and Son of God into a Hellenistic setting and very rapidly lost sight of the apocalyptic content of the former term and of the biblical, radically monotheistic context of the latter. The terms eventually were fastened to the two-nature language of the church's Christological formulae, and their original meaning was lost. Whereas Son of Man—particularly in the texts concerning the coming of the Son of Man on clouds of glory—indicates a heavenly figure of the end-times (and hardly a human "nature" like ours!), Son of God and "Son" used in relation to the divine Father most frequently indicate the close, filial relationship between Jesus and God, the relationship identified by Jesus' address to God as *"Abba,"* and the establishment of God's kingdom in and through Jesus, not a "divine nature" in Jesus. Jesus' divinity can better be inferred from other portions of the New Testament, like the *logos* language of John or the preexistence language of Paul.[9]

If doctrinal theology fails to pay attention to these results of exegesis and to their place in the Christological expositions of recent theologies of the New Testament, it will become guilty of perpetuating an exegetical error. We can no longer divine our dogmatic discussions of the person of Christ into sections dealing with Christ as Son of Man and as Son of God, as if those sections are sufficient and exhaustive presentations of his humanity and divinity. Nor can we easily press the traditional language of "person" and "natures" on to the biblical language as it is presently understood.

Indeed, doctrinal theology can learn from biblical theology to reorganize its discussion of Christology in terms of the

---

[8]Cf. J. Rodman Williams, *Renewal Theology*, 3 vols. (Grand Rapids: Zondervan, 1988–), 1:306, 328, 342.

[9]Cf. Oscar Cullmann, *Christology of the New Testament*, trans. Shirley Guthrie and Charles Hall (Philadelphia: Westminster, 1959), pp. 265–69, 270, 293–94.

New Testament "Jesus sayings" and the various names and titles of Christ, understood exegetically and historically. As a result it will have a firmer basis in the New Testament and will also provide a more substantial as well as more ecclesially useful foundation for the proclamation of Christ's humanity and divinity. In other words, a revision of the dogmatic *locus* of the person of Christ in terms of the results of New Testament theology does not set aside churchly teaching. Rather, it allows us to understand the church's dogmas in a new and, surely, clearer light.

We return to the fact that the construction and exposition of doctrinal or systematic theology is a hermeneutical task: the results of contemporary exegesis of Christological language like "Son of Man" and "Son of God," although different from the traditional usage, do not so much falsify the tradition as add another dimension to it by returning to the documents from which the tradition itself arose and by finding there a meaning that had been forgotten. Our contemporary restructuring of Christology retains both the fundamental issue of the humanity and divinity of Christ and the religious and theological value of past testimony to that issue, albeit in and through a use of biblical language different from our own. We must continue to refer to the tradition inasmuch as the tradition is the bearer of the gospel as a significant message to us.

Our doctrinal theology, then, cannot simply replace one usage with another. It must rather present and analyze the various usages, identifying with care why and how a contemporary exegetical result demands the reinterpretation of traditional language, but at the same time eliciting from the traditional language its underlying doctrinal and religious intention as of continuing significance in the community of belief. In other words, the patristic understanding of the New Testament language of "Son of Man" and "Son of God" may no longer be exegetically acceptable, but the religious and theological significance of that language, gained through the use of an exegetical method considerably different from our own, still bears scrutiny as a significant approach to the Christological problem, an approach from which we can learn in the present.

In addition, from a somewhat negative methodological perspective, it remains true that those who do not learn from history will simply repeat its mistakes. Much as a critical, historical exegetical method permits us to encounter a text or idea with a surer sense of its original meaning, so also does a critical approach to the historical materials of Christianity enable us to understand why we formulate our theology in particular ways—especially when those ways are different from the results of present-day exegesis. We live, in other words, not only with the results of our own exegesis, but with the results of the exegesis of the past. When those past results are held unexamined as doctrinal tenets, they can stand in the way of exegesis as easily as they can support it.

A perfect example of the function of historical materials in providing a secondary norm for doctrinal theology as well as an excellent example of the problem of past exegetical results impinging on contemporary exegesis is the doctrine of the Trinity. It was Bishop Gore who commented, toward the end of the last century, that the doctrine of the Trinity "is not so much heard as overheard" in the New Testament. Not only can we understand why the early church developed such a doctrine as the way of dealing with the problem of monotheism in the context of the affirmations of the divinity of Christ and of the Holy Spirit, we can also grasp the problem of the modern exegete who sees in the New Testament no language of divine essence and persons and who finds that virtually all of the texts referring to God as Father are not Trinitarian in character but rather intend simply to identify God in a close relationship with his creatures. Similarly, many of the texts that identify Jesus as the "Son" refer to Jesus in his humanity as one who stood in a close, "filial" relationship with God.

On the one hand, we must not allow our postbiblical Trinitarian terms to hide from us the meaning of the text. On the other hand, we ought not permit the difficulties brought to theology by modern exegesis to deprive us of a view of God—the doctrine of the Trinity—that provides a solution to the theological difficulties in such texts as the prologue to John or the various Pauline texts indicating Christ's heavenly preexistence and divinity. In its function as a secondary norm for Christian teaching, the doctrine of the Trinity supplies us with a cogent meditation on the essential relatedness of God and of the ability of God to relate in creation and redemption to the created order. The genius of the doctrine is that it presses on us the theological point that the agent of redemption is fully divine— not a secondary being who cannot ultimately draw humanity into relation with God. The doctrine has stood for so long because its fundamental intention is profoundly biblical and profoundly monotheistic; and in this sense it remains a guide to our exegesis. We are not required to press the Nicene doctrine into every nook and cranny of the text of the New Testament, but we ought to be very careful to maintain, in all of our exegesis, the recognition that Scripture, echoed in the church's doctrine, speaks to us of one God who is Creator and Redeemer.

Historical materials also provide paradigms and principles of organization for theology. A brief examination of modern theological systems bears this out. Very few systems of theology are original in their basic organization—nor is there any necessity that they should be, as long as the traditional patterns of organization continue to serve the biblical and historical materials of theology and the needs of the present-day community of faith. (It has been, moreover, a standard practice in systems of theology and studies of "theological encyclopedia" written in a classical or traditional teaching style to incorporate short histories of the discipline in their prolegomena—so that basic information about the historical development of theological system is readily available and can easily be incorporated into contemporary study.)[10]

---

[10]In, e.g., Louis Berkhof, *Introduction to Systematic Theology* (Grand Rapids: Eerdmans, 1932; repr. Grand Rapids: Baker, 1979); George R. Crooks and John F. Hurst, *Theological Encyclopaedia and Methodology*, new ed., rev. (New York: Hunt and Eaton, 1894). Christoph Luthardt, *Kompendium der Dogmatik*, 11th posthumous ed. (Leipzig: Dörfling & Franke, 1914); Philip Schaff, *Theological Propaedeutic: a General Introduction to the Study of Theology, Exegetical, Historical, Systematic, and Practical* (New York: Scribner, 1894); Otto Weber, *Foundations of Dogmatics*, trans. Darrell Guder, 2 vols. (Grand Rapids: Eerdmans, 1981–82);

By way of example, the basic paradigm followed by such diverse thinkers as Thomas Aquinas, John Calvin, Johann Gerhard, Francis Turretin, Karl Barth, J. T. Mueller, Louis Berkhof, and Carl Braaten moves from an initial declaration of the grounds of theology to a doctrine of God and creation, to a discussion of the human predicament and the work of redemption in Christ, to a presentation of such topics as church, sacraments, and the last things. Order may vary from system to system, but the basic pattern of four groupings of topics—prolegomena, theology, anthropology and soteriology, ecclesiology and eschatology—is present in all of the theological systems mentioned. We can trace the pattern back to the *Sentences* of Peter Lombard (d. 1160) and from there to the treatise *On the Orthodox Faith* of John of Damascus (d. 754).

The question confronting contemporary systematic theology, of course, is whether or not the traditional form still serves adequately the presentation of the body of Christian doctrine—whether, in fact, the preliminary examination of the character, sources, and methods of theology that ought to precede any system of theology now demands the alteration not only of detail but also of basic patterns of organization. In the nineteenth century, the Kantian interpretation of religion as grounded on ethics led to the ethical interpretation of the Christian hope, with the result that a radical eschatology is lacking from Albrecht Ritschl's theology. In addition, the assumption of many nineteenth-century thinkers that theology could and ought to be focused on certain fundamental or principial doctrines led to the structural revision of systems: Alexander Schweizer centered his theology on the divine causality and our dependence on it; Gottfried Thomasius focused his entire system on the doctrine of the person and work of Christ; Albrecht Ritschl produced an entire theology under the rubric of "justification and reconciliation." Should we today, for example, follow the realization that the New Testament preaching of Jesus is guided by a thoroughly

Revere Franklin Weidner, *Introduction to Dogmatic Theology, Based on Luthardt* (Rock Island, Ill.: Augustana Book Concern, 1888).

eschatological perspective to a new form of theology centered on "the last things"?[11] Or should we, granting the difficulty of confronting God-language in the twentieth century, find some beginning point for a theological system other than discussions of revelation, Scripture, and God—perhaps a phenomenology of religion in general, or a philosophical discussion of the grounds of religion.

PHILOSOPHICAL APPROACHES AND THE STUDY OF RELIGION

If the problems and directions of theological system in our day point in the direction of philosophical and phenomenological approaches to religion, it is also true that philosophical theology and the closely related disciplines of the philosophy and phenomenology of religion are subjects that strain at the bounds of the traditional fourfold encyclopedia and which, in fact, belong in part to theological study and in part to secular academic study. These subjects straddle the fence, so to speak, between the sacred and the secular. Without implying a pejorative view of either subject and while affirming the necessity of both to the contemporary formulation of theology, both may be said to view the sacred from a generalized point of view that stands within the bounds of no particular theological or religious community. In so doing, both philosophical theology and philosophy of religion stand in a position over against doctrinal theology that is at once propaedeutic and critical.

Philosophical theology can be defined as the philosophical discussion of topics held in common by theology and philosophy. This means that philosophical theology would discuss the existence, essence, and attributes of God but not the doctrine of the Trinity; it would discuss the problem of evil but not the doctrines of sin and grace. Whereas the topics of this discipline come from both theology and philosophy and mark out the

---

[11]Cf. Thomas N. Finger, *Christian Theology: An Eschatological Approach*, 2 vols. (Scottsdale, Pa.: Herald, 1985–89).

common subject of both, the methodology comes from philosophy and focuses on questions of knowledge and being—epistemology and ontology. As over against theology, or more specifically, "Christian" or "revealed" theology, philosophical theology, in order to be true to itself, must not utilize Scripture or churchly standards of truth: it rests on the truths of logic and reason—and occupies the ground of what has typically been called "natural theology." In this sense, philosophical theology provides a logical and rational check on dogmatic formulation. Philosophy of religion, by way of contrast, considers the nature of religion itself a focus that it shares with the phenomenology of religion.

From a propaedeutic or "preparatory" perspective, both philosophical theology and philosophy of religion stand as points of transition between purely philosophical study and the study of theology. In order to think theologically with any precision, one needs to be able to deal with basic categories of philosophy as they come to bear on the questions of knowing and of being. Thus philosophical theology has an interest in the broad questions of knowledge of God, including the traditional proofs of God's existence; in issues concerning the nature of language about God; in the discussion of human nature and human destiny; in the relation of God and world; and in the problem of evil. Philosophical theology is the discipline of basic questions—so that here also we take up, as a philosophical question, the feasibility of theology as an academic discipline, as examined in Pannenberg's *Theology and the Philosophy of Science*.[12]

There is also, and equally importantly, a critically constructive function of philosophical theology and philosophy of religion within the framework of systematics. These two subject areas belong to the study of theology and to the theological curriculum precisely because they ask the broad, foundational questions necessary to the existence of theology as a discipline. There are also two basic locations for these subject

---

[12]Wolfhart Pannenberg, *Theology and the Philosophy of Science*, trans. Francis McDonagh (Philadelphia: Westminster, 1976).

areas within the larger historical/constructive pattern of theology: both philosophical theology and philosophy of religion can be treated historically and both can be treated synthetically or constructively. In the former case, they parallel the biblical and church historical studies as ancillary fields devoted to the creation of a proper context for understanding the historical progress of the Judeo-Christian religion and its theology. In the latter case they provide a conceptual framework for dealing with the religious and the philosophical elements that belong to the contemporary expression of Christianity. Both of these locations are legitimate. What is more, they are mutually enlightening and ought to be held simultaneously in view as one of the grounds of the interpretive unity of theology.

The term *philosophical theology* denotes a more intimate relationship between philosophy and theology than obtains in the other subdisciplines and, what is more important to the definition, the determination of the topics and contents of theology by another set of interest and competencies, the philosophical. For philosophical theology clearly cannot deal with issues that are incapable of philosophical treatment. This fact makes philosophical theology unique among the "systematic" disciplines: it is the only one of the subdisciplines grouped together as "systematic theology" the structure of which is determined by a nontheological discipline, a discipline external to the circle of the theological encyclopedia.

The very name "philosophical theology" implies something negative about the relationship of philosophy and theology: it implies that not all theology is philosophical, that the relationship is not a necessary one, and, by extension, that some forms of theology may find an element of their identity and reason for being in the fact that they are not at all philosophical. We have already encountered one of those forms in the discipline or subdiscipline "biblical theology" and its divisions "Old Testament theology" and "New Testament theology." Even when biblical theology implies no particular antagonism for other theological disciplines, like philosophical or doctrinal theology, it does imply an exclusion of purely philosophical (or doctrinal) categories from its presuppositions and essential structures or definitions for the sake of an exclusive reliance on the theological categories provided by the text of Scripture. Biblical theology can, however, be juxtaposed with both philosophical and doctrinal theology as a genre unaffected by categories extraneous and therefore inimical to the biblical revelation.

Philosophical theology is distinct from philosophy of religion. There is, of course, considerable common ground: both disciplines deal with the concepts of God, good and evil, human nature, and human destiny. The difference between the disciplines, even in this area of common interest, is the more purely phenomenological perspective of the philosophy of religion: here the philosophical concern predominates to the point that all religion becomes the phenomenon under investigation and the Christian perspective, if present, will need to be justified phenomenologically. Philosophical theology, however, so long as it stands within the circle of the theological encyclopedia, must be a Christian discipline, no matter how philosophically determined its contents. Topics proper to philosophy of religion, such as primitive religion and the origin of religious belief, magic, and ritual, cannot properly belong to philosophical theology. Philosophy of religion has a profound interest in comparative religion—whereas philosophical theology does not.

This typology, no more than any other, falls short of perfection when we move from theory to actuality. There are quite a few words the titles of which blur the lines we have drawn between philosophical theology and philosophy of religion. One work in particular that comes to mind is Fairbairn's *Philosophy of the Christian Religion*.[13] This work, one of the major theoretical expositions of Christianity from the early part of this century, contains a fully developed comparative philosophy of religion within the structure of a Christian philosophical theology—it is interested both in the comparison of religions and in the philosophical examination of Christianity

---

[13]Andrew M. Fairbairn, *The Philosophy of the Christian Religion* (New York: Macmillan, 1902).

as the highest and the true religion. There can, in short, be such a thing as a Christian philosophy of religion, just as there can be a non-Christian philosophical theology. But the basic typology holds insofar as philosophy of religion must encompass the whole phenomenon of religion and encounter beliefs other than the Christian, while philosophical theology, when written from a Christian perspective will not be an essay in comparative religion.

Philosophy of religion is a broader topic than philosophical theology, just as "religion" is a broader category than "theology." Here religion in general is the subject and, in addition to the purely philosophical issues of epistemology and ontology, the methodology of comparative religion or "history of religions" must be brought to bear. John Caird, the British idealist, commented in his *Introduction to the Philosophy of Religion*:

> There is no province of human experience, there is nothing in the whole realm of reality, which lies beyond the domain of philosophy, or to which philosophical investigation does not extend. Religion, so far from forming an exception to the all-embracing sphere of philosophy, is rather just that province which lies nearest to it, for, in one point of view religion and philosophy have common objects and a common content.[14]

In the spirit of grasping "the whole realm of reality," philosophy examines religion and finds that it cannot be confined to the Christian religion but must examine the phenomenon of human religiosity.

By placing philosophy of religion into the context of the constructive or systematizing effort, we in no way mean to de-emphasize its historical and critical importance. The study of religion, in the first place, has become in our times a crucial adjunct to exegesis. As Ebeling comments,

> We meet a multitude of foreign religions within the Old and New Testaments, such as, for example, the Canaanite cults vis-

---

[14]John Caird, *An Introduction to the Philosophy of Religion* (New York: Macmillan, 1881), p. 3.

à-vis Israel or the Hellenistic cults as counterparts of primitive Christianity. The worship of the true God necessarily conflicts with the worship of false gods, and the gospel with any other message of salvation. Biblical, Christian faith cannot be expressed apart from polemical contact with the world of the religions. It is also apparent in the biblical texts that faith in Yahweh as well as in Christ is susceptible to foreign influences.[15]

In other words, the study of religions provides the context for understanding both the formation and the contextualization of Israelite and Christian religion. Without some grasp of this context there can be little understanding, for example, of how the originally Palestinian phenomenon of Christianity was able to adapt its expression of the gospel to the thought-forms of the Graeco-Roman world and become over the course of time the world religion that it is today.

In addition, without this contextualized understanding of the forms of the Christian message, we can easily fall into the trap of moving from the thought-world of the first century to the thought-world of the twentieth as if a process of interpretation and recontextualization were unnecessary. When that incredibly erudite exponent of late nineteenth-century German liberalism, Adolf von Harnack, endeavored to explain "the essence of Christianity"[16]—having first dispensed with the historical Hellenization of doctrine and, indeed, the entire history of dogma—he brought on himself the stinging critique of having ignored history and having found his own theology in the New Testament rather than the teaching of the New Testament itself. In George Tyrrell's words, Harnack had looked down the well of history and had seen a liberal Postestant face reflected back at him.[17]

In the light of these considerations, we must differ with Ebeling's pronouncement that "through religious studies theology is neither increased by a further discipline nor supplement-

---

[15]Ebeling, *The Study of Theology*, p. 39.

[16]Adolf von Harnack, *What is Christianity*, trans. Thomas Saunders intro. by Rudolf Bultmann (New York: Harper & Row, 1957).

[17]George Tyrrell, *Christianity at the Cross-Roads* (London: Longmans, Green, 1910), p. 44.

ed by a discipline outside of theology, but is rather placed in question as such."[18] On the one hand, religious studies that take as their subject the phenomenon of religion in general do in fact constitute a disciplinary augmentation of theology as it has traditionally been understood. On the other hand, such general studies of the phenomenon cannot—and in a methodological sense *ought* not—call in question the normative expression of any particular religion. (It is one of the curious features of American academic life that Buddhism and Hinduism are permitted to be taught as value-systems from which truth can be learned and self-understanding gained, while the similar teaching of Christianity in the university or secular college context is deemed a violation of canons of objectivity or denial of the salutary separation of "church" and "state"!)

The study of religions can provide the proper phenomenological context for the understanding of a normative Christianity. It is one of the negative elements of the heritage of neoorthodoxy that religion and revelation are severed and Christianity is cut off from religion in general. Such thinking, while seemingly affirmative of the absoluteness and uniqueness of the Christian message, actually serves to cut the ground out from under Christianity. By defining Christianity alone as based on revelation and by viewing human religiosity, generally and phenomenologically conceived, as either simply error or as having nothing to do with the way in which we understand our Christianity or frame our theology, neoorthodoxy left Christianity open to the standard rationalistic critiques of revelation and of theological language. At the same time it removes the broad justification of Christianity as one of the higher forms (arguably the highest!) of the general and genuine human apprehension of the divine as the ultimate and necessary element in a coherent construction of reality. In the final analysis, the neoorthodox approach to religion and revelation reduces to an obscurantist ploy that avoids a series of difficult phenomenological and historical questions rather than trying to answer them.

[18]Ebeling, *The Study of Theology*, p. 40.

ETHICS AND APOLOGETICS

In addressing the movement of theological formulation from its biblical, historical, and philosophical roots toward ethics and apologetics, we are in fact anticipating the next two sections of our discussion—the relation of statement to practice and the work of formulation in the present. Both ethics and apologetics function as theological disciplines on the boundary between theory and practice, each having a theoretical pole consisting in formal statement and a practical or active pole consisting in an address to the present situation that demands active result. This boundary-character of the disciplines has led, in various of the older "encyclopedias," to their discussion either as practical or systematic disciplines, and either as component parts of or as adjuncts to dogmatic theology— manifesting, if nothing else, the problem of the "diversified encyclopedia" in the organization and study of theology.

This problem of the relationship of ethics and apologetics to the other disciplines indicates also a problem of formulation in the disciplines of ethics and apologetics themselves: Do they function independently? do they rest directly on Scripture? or do they draw their principles and materials from other disciplines, and if so which ones? In the case of ethics, this is a fairly old debate, extending back at least to the sixteenth century, when the question arose whether or not there ought to be Christian ethics, distinct from the philosophical ethics based on Aristotle. Quite a few Reformed theologians understood dogmatics and ethics—faith and works, or obedience—to constitute the basic divisions of doctrinal theology. The renewed study of Aristotle and, to a certain extent, the strict division between teachings concerning the faith and teachings concerning obedience led to the eventual separation of the disciplines of dogmatics and ethics. This separation was strengthened at the close of the eighteenth century by Kant's derivation of religion from ethics—making ethics a foundational discipline, not controlled by principles drawn from religion and not to be fashioned on the basis of a system of dogmatic theology, itself derived from ethics by way of religion.

Several American theologians of the last century attempted to overcome this separation by identifying ethics as a subdivision of doctrinal theology: the Methodist theologian Miner Raymond presented an entire ethical system within his *Systematic Theology*.[19] Charles Hodge and Robert Dabney attempted, somewhat less successfully, to deal with ethics under the rubric of the Ten Commandments, within a somewhat catechetically ordered system of theology.[20] For the most part, however, theologians of the nineteenth and twentieth centuries have allowed the separation of the disciplines, leaving us with the question of their relationship with each other and with the other disciplines within the larger study of theology.

In the first place, it should be clear that ethics does not simply deal with "things to be done," in the highly useful and instructive language of scholasticism, the *agenda*, but also and in some sense prior to the agenda, with "things to be believed" or *credenda*. It should also be clear—inasmuch as it is historically and phenomenologically correct—that the basic principles known to Judeo-Christian ethics by the investigation of the biblical revelation are also known to Western philosophy, to the "higher" religions, and to "natural reason." There is, in other words, a kinship between the principles of a purely "biblical" ethics based on the Decalogue, a philosophical ethics drawn from "natural reason," and a religious ethics learned from Buddhism, Hinduism, or Confucianism. (This point reinforces the point made previously about the importance of the study not only of philosophy but also of the history and phenomenology of religion as disciplines collateral to theology.)

We must, however, disagree with Ebeling's argument that ethics "treats what is purely human because it deals with the behavior and actions of people on their own responsibility, cast upon themselves as though there were no God."[21] The general acceptance and multiple sources of ethical principles and the

---

[19]Miner Raymond, *Systematic Theology* 2 vols. (New York: Eaton and Mains, 1892–94).

[20]Cf. the comments in Berkhof, *Introduction*, pp. 50–51.

[21]Ebeling, *The Study of Theology*, p. 139.

utterly concrete address and application of ethics ought not to be understood as making ethics any less a theological discipline. Christian ethics—indeed, a religious ethics generally understood—must stand in contrast to those few systems of philosophical ethics that rule the divine out of consideration. Theological ethics arises in the context and is built on the terms set by our creatureliness. (This context and foundation leads, in the formulation of ethics, to the same kind of biblical, historical, philosophical, and phenomenological richness that we found to obtain in the formulation of doctrinal theology and provides, as well, a theological basis for the inclusion of the results of philosophical, phenomenological, and history-of-religions investigation in our ethical formulations.)

The ethical task is nothing less than the translation of the materials of Christian teaching—whether biblical, historical, doctrinal, or philosophical—into the contemporary life situation of the community of belief, first as principles and then as enactments. This task demands, as in the case of doctrinal theology, close attention to interpretive questions concerning the relationship between the situation in which the original ethical statement or principle was operative and the contemporary situation—together with close attention to the question of whether a particular standard is *apodictic*, expressing a necessary truth, or *casuistic*, expressing a prudent solution to a particular issue.

By way of example, certain of the mandates in the Levitical Code have long been recognized by the church as belonging legitimately to the life of ancient Israel but equally as not transferable to the contemporary situation. Not only can we recognize that the sacrificial aspects of the Code have been superceded in and for the church by Christ's work of atonement, but also we are forced, historically, to note the absence of a temple at which to sacrifice. Our theological and historical situation does not require observance: these commands must be regarded as casuistic. A somewhat different issue confronts us in the case of commands such as the death penalty by stoning in cases of adultery. Whereas we can understand—particularly with the aid of social anthropology—the need of smaller societies to have more stringent forms of social control, and we can also understand, in the case of ancient Israel, the confluence of religious with social controls in an essentially theocratic state, yielding a basic equation of religious ethic with civil law, we must also recognize the rather different situation of our own society. In our contemporary social situation, the religious and the civil are separate, agreeing in some points but not in others. Religious authorities no longer have the power of life and death, and religiously grounded ethical codes do not directly demand civil action. The difference between our contemporary context and the Old Testament context demonstrates that this particular aspect of the law, also, cannot be counted as apodictic. Nonetheless, the law against adultery itself—apart from the question of penalties—remains within the context of the apodictic law, granting that the moral and personal impact of the breakdown of marriage is not limited to a particular historical context. Ethics, thus, must be a practical but not an utterly pragmatic discipline: it points toward enactment or praxis, but it maintains at the same time certain absolute standards in and through its response to all situations.

As has frequently been observed, apologetics is the oldest kind of formally conceived Christian theology, dating from the works of the so-called Greek apologists of the mid-second century. From that point onward, it has been a discipline that has argued both the philosophical and the ethical excellence of Christianity both in terms of the teachings of Scripture and the church and in terms of the standards set, external to Christianity, both by philosophy and by other religions.

The questions that we noted concerning the relationship of ethics to the other disciplines thus also obtain in the discussion of apologetics. "Apologetics," of course, indicates a defense of the faith and not at all a case of second thoughts— being "sorry" for one's beliefs. The discipline of apologetic theology represents the logical and rational defense of the principles and truths of the Christian religion. The topics of apologetics, therefore, relate directly to the contents both of philosophical and of doctrinal theology, with the intention of manifesting those contents to be believable and even compelling in the face of skepticism or disbelief.

This task is, in a sense, precisely the opposite of the task of philosophical theology considered as a propaedeutic and critical discipline. Whereas philosophical theology brings to bear critical faculties on theology by moving from the secular to the sacred, apologetic theology brings critical faculties to bear on unbelief by moving—with the prior development of philosophical and doctrinal theology well in hand—from the sacred to the secular. Because of the logical and critical approach necessary to this discipline, it has frequently been developed, particularly in more empirically oriented works, as a study in the "evidences of Christianity."[22]

The question of the place of apologetics in theological study arises out of the nature of apologetics in relation to doctrinal theology: Is it a prolegomenon to or a result of dogmatics? Does the defensive discipline precede and make a case for the viability of the declarative discipline, or does it follow, and on the basis of a prior declaration of faith, argue the truth of the essential articles of Christian doctrine? The answer to these questions determines not only the scope of apologetics but also the patterns of argument and interpretation belonging to the discipline itself. The issue has been one of the most pointed addressed internally by Reformed theology during the last two centuries. Philip Schaff, the two Hodges, and Benjamin B. Warfield placed apologetics first as a prolegomenon or propaedeutic and limited its function to the general "proof" of the perfection or rectitude of Christianity, excluding both doctrinal discussion and "denominational differences" from apologetics correctly so called.[23] Defense of specific doctrinal points, according to these theologians, would belong to "polemics," which is seldom taught as a discipline in the twentieth century. This view of apologetics stands in continuity

---

[22]See, for example, George P. Fisher, *The Grounds of Theistic and Christian Belief* (New York: Scribner, 1883) and idem., *Christian Evidences* (New York: Macmillan, 1882).

[23]Cf. Schaff, *Theological Propaedeutic*, p. 311.

with the function given to the discipline in Schleiermacher's *Brief Outline*, where it is identified as a fundamental form of philosophical theology, prior in function to the historical-exegetical disciplines.[24] However, the Dutch Reformed school—Kuyper and Bavinck and, in America, Berkhof and Van Til—insisted that apologetics follow dogmatics even as reason, when used in theology, must take its point of departure from faith. And since, in their view, dogmatics itself rested on the biblical and historical disciplines, apologetics would naturally come at the very conclusion of the work of theological formulation or of theological study—and would absorb the task of polemics.

A partial answer to the question of placement and significance, not altogether satisfying to either of these groups, can be gathered from the interpretive context of the apologetic task and from the use to which apologetic treatises have been put in particular ages of the church. In the second century, the age of the first and arguably the greatest apologetic effort of the Christian church, a series of treatises that argued the ethical purity of the Christian religion and the philosophical superiority of its monotheism were addressed by a series of philosophically trained converts to the Roman emperors Hadrian, Antoninus Pius, and Marcus Aurelius. The documents, on the surface, were designed as pleas to these judicious and philosophically minded emperors to hear the case of the persecuted Christians and to deal justly with their situation: the rectitude of their lives and the high philosophical monotheism advocated by the Christians deserved tolerance, not persecution. Here is a fundamental, preliminary apologetic.

Yet, as one major patristic scholar has pointed out, the address to the emperor may only be a literary device, and the documents may have been used primarily as missionary documents directed to near-converts at the edge of the community or to newly converted Christians in doubt about the substance of the new religion. Here we cross over from

---

[24]Friedrich Schleiermacher, *A Brief Outline of the Study of Theology* (Atlanta, Ga.: John Knox, 1966), pp. 32–35.

preliminary apologetic into the realm of the defense of the faith, replete with the lengthy, often highly developed examination of Christian beliefs. The same documents functioned, potentially, in two different ways. Beyond this, as anyone who has studied the history of Christian doctrine knows, whatever the intention of the authors of these documents, their doctrinal arguments contributed to the development of early Trinitarianism and to the rise of *logos* Christology.

In the interpretive history of the Christian community, apologetics rises out of theological conviction and passes back into theology, influencing its formulation. As in the case of the broader history of doctrine—the forward temporal motion, as it were, of doctrinal theology—so also in the case of apologetics does the present formulation arise out of the biblical-churchly tradition, drawing on the basic assumptions of the original proclamation of the gospel as interpreted in and through the ongoing religious life of the believing community. What is defended, however unchanged its central focus on the Christ-event, constantly changes in response to the language, the needs, and the problems of new historical contexts.

The form and use of apologetics, therefore, draws both on the biblical and historical tradition of teaching and on the contemporary situation. Apologetics rests on the presupposition of faith or belief and never stands entirely outside of the other disciplines—i.e., it cannot be presuppositionless and absolutely preparatory or foundational—but its actual content must be dictated as much by the circumstances of the argument as by the content of the message. Thus the apologetic task may involve the defense of foundational issues such as the existence of God, or it may involve the discussion of the exegesis of biblical texts or even the appropriateness of various methods of interpretation to the task of exegesis. In each case, the apologetic task is an essentially interpretive function of the believing community in the present as the community interacts with its situation in the world.

Ethics and apologetics, taken together, are in fact the place where the success or failure of our biblical, historical, and systematic study of theology becomes most obvious. If all we have done in our study is absorb a large amount of discrete and unrelated data, then the end result of our intellectual and spiritual pilgrimage will not be a religious or theological construction of reality—and it will not make sense ethically or apologetically of the world-order around us or of our place in it.

Ethics, after all, is not simply about abstract values. Ethics is about the correlation between values understood on the level of absolutes with the positive and constructive effect of the application of those values to concrete situations. A decisively Christian ethic will agree with classical philosophical ethics that value must be located in or identified as the absolute good—but it will add, as some but not all philosophical ethicists have argued, that this absolute good is God. If this identification is provided by doctrinal and philosophical theology, it is certainly put into its practical framework by ethics, where it becomes a practical guide for the identification of human beings as moral agents capable of responsible action.

At the level of making practical sense out of our world, it is the task of ethics to deal with such problems as the frequent absence of any immediate correlation between good conduct and good fortune in this life. The great problem, here, which Kant rightly identified, is not merely the problem of a simplistic ethical hedonism, in which good is identified as that which brings happiness. More than this, it is the problem of the correlation of the internal moral order with the external world-order. As Kant rightly saw, ethics must rest on religion, and God is a necessary postulate of the ethical. What a Christian ethics must do is inculcate value not only as a series of demands but as part of a religious construction of reality that identifies the good with God and, derivatively, with God's work.

On a very practical level, this identification manifests ecology and ecologically positive behavior as central issues for Christian ethics today. If the world as created is itself a value, our ethical conduct must involve the conservation of the natural order and the cultivation of the proper place of humanity in our world—not only in terms of empirically demonstrable goals that, however convincingly stated, will always be debated or abated out of various economic or corporate interests, but also and primarily in terms of the non–empirically verifiable identification of God and the divine purpose as the ultimate good.

We can note here the correlation of the results of contemporary exegesis both with theological formulation and with practical ethical need. Both against those critics of Christianity who have rightly noted the tendency of Western Christians to think that the gift of dominion (Gen. 1:28) was a gift of license, but who have wrongly seen this as the genuine meaning of the text, and against those Christians who have used the text as a ground for abusing nature, we can point to a fundamentally different implication of the words of Scripture. The gift of dominion in verse 28 clearly parallels and is defined by the creation of human beings in the image of God in verse 27. We know from archaeological and linguistic study that the bestowing of the image of a lord or ruler was a typical sign, in the concrete political life of the ancient world, of the bestowing of the powers of a viceroy and of the identification not of an abdication but of an extension of the power of the ruler. The viceroy bears the power but also the responsibility of conserving the ruler's property. The dominion of Genesis 1 relates very closely to the imagery of Genesis 2, where the newly created Adam is placed into the role of gardener-caretaker in the earthly paradise of Eden. The ethical implication of the exegesis is clear.

Apologetics similarly stands in a concrete and directly relevant relationship to the Christian task of making sense of life in this world. When apologetics, for instance, argues the cogency of religious language and the validity of the fundamental religious experience of the existence of God, it is not merely engaging in a philosophical task. True, much of the formal argumentation comes from philosophical theology, but, unlike philosophical theology, apologetics is arguing not only a theory but also and primarily a view of the world in which all things stand under and are responsible to a knowing Ultimate. If apologetics does indeed presuppose a body of belief, then its defensive argumentation takes on a highly existential significance: what is at stake in the apologetical discussion of the existence of God is the foundational truth concerning the higher reality on which all existence, all value, and all hope depend, and in terms of which all that we do ultimately makes sense.

If, as I have indicated from the outset of this book, theology is the "science of the Christian religion," the formal discipline that clarifies and codifies the meaning offered by the religion, then the ethical and apologetical tasks mark the point at which the interpretive argument comes full circle and the abstractive, discursive work of drawing meanings out of the documents and the life of the religion and working toward formulation of their contemporary significance returns to the religion with positive result. Ethics and apologetics, as disciplines at the boundary of theory and practice, take the results of the other theological disciplines and return them to the concrete life of the believing community.

THE RELATION OF STATEMENT TO PRACTICE

The effective relation of theological statement or formulation to churchly practice stands as one of the great problems of the church today. It is not at all untypical for expert "practitioners" of ministry—like the individual mentioned in the preface to this book—to have virtually no use for theology in the classical sense; and for expert "theologians" to have either very little contact with churchly practice or, when they do have the contact, very little liking for the style and substance of the practice. That there ought to be a positive relationship between statement and practice ought to be obvious. A Christianity that operates on a "do as I say, don't do as I do" or a "do as I do, ignore what I say" basis has not long to live. Our conception of God and God's work ought to make sense in terms of our practice—and our practice ought to support what we think about God and God's work.

One of the great maxims of the theological tradition, forgotten or set aside in the contemporary failure of theological study, is *lex orandi, lex credendi*: "The rule of praying [is] rule of believing." Our prayers, our worship services, our counseling, and our personal development as Christians all ought to fall into a theological pattern following the same fundamental rule as our doctrinal statements. Much of the problem experienced in the church arises, as Farley recognized, from the mistaken or partial identification of the practical; specifically, I would add, from the assumption that the classical or "theoretical" and "academic" theological disciplines are not "practical" or directly related to such theologically ill-defined contemporary goals as "equipping for ministry," "leadership training," and "church growth"—as if one can be properly equipped, trained as a leader, or pastor a church that is large for the right reasons without any knowledge of the substance of the faith or the disciplines designed to help interpret that substance!

Practical theology today is such a diverse field, with so many subdisciplines, so many partially identified areas of study seeking disciplinary status, and so many specialized ministerial tasks, that it echoes the general problem of the "diversified encyclopedia" within its own smaller compass. In addition to the traditional disciplines of worship or liturgy, homiletics, and counseling, we can also count spirituality or personal formation, various kinds of teaching and group study, youth ministry, marriage and family ministry, geriatric ministry, and so forth. All of these specializations and more would have to be enumerated if the point of our discussion were to outline specialized techniques—but our purpose is precisely the opposite. The task that confronts us is the analysis of practical theology in its widest sense, in relation to the study of theology and the unity of theological knowing. Specifically, the task before us is the relation of the so-called theoretical disciplines to practice as biblical, historical, and systematic theology are brought to bear on the life of the church.

The argument put forth previously that all theology is both theoretical and practical also applies to the field of "practical theology." Inasmuch as practical theology is *theology* and a category for the gathering together of several theological subdisciplines, it brings with it both the theoretical considerations characteristic of its separate disciplines and the theological *praxis*, the orientation toward the goal of salvation that is characteristic of all the theological disciplines, including the so-called theoretical ones. The point is important, granting the frequently made mistake of identifying ministerial or pastoral theology with practice and historical or systematic theology with theory—as if the former were never theoretical and the latter never practical.

Ebeling reflects on the contemporary bias toward the "practical" in his comment, "It is characteristic of modern times that theory is valid only in relationship to practice."[25] The point is well taken, if rightly understood. And it relates directly to the emphasis on history and religion present throughout our discussion. The church's "theory," its theological formulation, has never arisen, except in very recent times, apart from the religious life of the believing community. This is not only a fundamental fact of church history, it is also a fundamental fact of the biblical witness. The process of corporate reflection that brought together the canon of Scripture was in no small part a verification of the message of the prophets and the apostles in and through the religious life, the practice of the community. A similar point can very easily be made concerning the church's worship: except for the usually less-than-successful attempts of modern denominational worship committees to produce "new liturgy," the practice of the church has been to develop forms of worship in and through the practice of worship. Prayers, creeds, and hymns become set forms only after long development and use. Theological formulae, particularly in the early church, ultimately became normative only when they were understood as constructive or supportive of the teaching of salvation as offered in worship. It is widely recognized that the defeat of Arianism in the fourth century had virtually as much to do with the church's adherence to a Trinitarian reading of the baptismal formula (Matt. 28:19) as it did with detailed theological discussion.

No one would claim, either historically or presently, that theory absolutely precedes practice. It is true, however, that theory typically precedes coherent practice—and that knowledge of biblical, historical, and systematic theology precedes coherent ministry in and for the church. The several practical

---

[25]Ebeling, *The Study of Theology*, p. 116.

disciplines teach this point as clearly as do any of the theoretical disciplines. Homiletics has, perhaps longer than any of the other divisions of practical theology, had a clear method of approach. Whether one is taught to develop "three-point" sermons, or to argue in an expository fashion directly on the text of Scripture, or to work out, in a manner similar to the Puritan preachers of the seventeenth century, a carefully conceived doctrinal or moral treatise resting, with the proper balance of emphases, on Scripture and reason, the coherence of what is preached clearly rests on a method of moving from the text through interpretation, to the point of delivery. And, as experience demonstrates to anyone who has attempted to preach, coherent practice does rest on some grasp of the theory, not only of exegesis, interpretation, and theological formulation, but also of the task of preaching.

A similar example can be drawn from the somewhat newer discipline of pastoral counseling. The counseling work of the Christian minister—the care and cure of souls—has always been a part of the ministerial task, but only in this century has it become a fully developed discipline. The rise of the discipline of pastoral counseling has to do in large measure with the rise of psychology and the increased understanding provided by psychology of the inner problems faced by individuals, of the meaning and dynamics of personal existence in relation to other persons, and of various ways of analyzing personal problems, counseling persons through their difficulties, of initiating therapeutic interventions with persons, and, indeed, of modifying behavior.

As Seward Hiltner well argued in several of his groundbreaking essays, clinical pastoral training and pastoral psychology have rightly "stressed their connection with and indebtedness to psychotherapy, and the other life sciences and technologies."[26] Hiltner went on to argue for the further development of a genuine pastoral *theology* that would have much the same

[26]Seward Hiltner, "Pastoral Thand Psychology," in Arnold S. Nash, ed., *Protestant Thought in the Twentieth Century: Whence and Whither* (New York: Macmillan, 1951), p. 196.

content as pastoral psychology but would have "a different frame of reference" and would see its "content in a different context."[27]

As in the case of ethics, so also in pastoral counseling, the Christian context implies a theological framework of meaning in which the individual is understood as standing within God's world—but here, not so much in terms of right relationship to the world order as in terms of right relationship with other persons and right construction of patterns of behavior. What is distinctively Christian here is the conviction concerning values and norms and the assumption that these values and norms arise not as projections of self, but as truths about the self and its relationships given by God and belonging, therefore, to the fabric of the world order.

If placed into the context of modern psychology, pastoral counseling will have as much of a problem with the soul as most psychological theory does. Psychology, despite the etymology of its name, has little use for the concept of soul and of ultimate values associated with the traditional theological and philosophical meditations on the soul. Typically, psychology, of its very nature, studies the phenomenal order and looks either toward measurable evidence, such as patterns of brain waves, or toward quantifiable data, such as the behavior of certain types of persons. The categories of psychological analysis and counseling are drawn, therefore, out of the phenomenal order and relate directly to practice. There is a profound—and necessary—pragmatism in much of the work of psychology.

This means, however, that such techniques as transactional analysis or behavior modification are not designed to raise philosophical questions, particularly questions concerning reality and value. Transactional analysis, for example, understands individuals in terms of the "child," the "adult," and the "parent" that are "in" the individual—because these categories *work* in analysis and counseling. As far as I know, however, this approach never asks the question of the nature of these

---

[27]Ibid., pp. 196-97.

categories: Are they really or only formally or rationally distinct—i.e., should they be viewed as mutually exclusive "things" or are they merely functions? If they do not have the status of "thing," of *what* are they functions? Or, are there other possible categories—such as "sibling," "adolescent," "aunt/uncle"—and if not, why not? And finally, is there any moral value assignable to any of these categories or related to their functions as aspects of a larger "psychical" (i.e., soulish or spiritual) reality in and of the individual? Similarly, behavior modification refrains from asking the questions of value and seeks, simply, to alter the patterns of a person's behavior by means of a therapy involving positive and negative inducements or stimuli.

When pastoral counseling draws on these various psychological perspectives and uses their techniques in ministry, it must also ask the theological and philosophical questions that do not and cannot belong to psychological science as it is presently constituted. Ministry, of its very nature, deals with values, absolutes, and ultimates as identified by and in Christianity. Far from being merely a speculative or philosophical question, the question of the soul marks the point at which the consideration of values and absolutes comes into view—because it identifies an orientation of the person that rises above the animal, the visceral, and the sexual and that lodges value on a "higher" plane than individual or social self-interest. Discussion of "soul," unlike discussion of behavior and its modification, raises questions concerning the identification of the good and the true—and it presses standards of behavior toward the ultimate.[28] Pastoral counseling, because of its rootage beyond itself in the biblical, historical, and systematic theological disciplines must rest on such concepts.

What remains for the practical disciplines, therefore, once they have mastered their own internal theories—whether of the

---

[28]This problem is not merely a churchly or theological problem; it is clearly described from the purely secular academic and societal point of view by Allan Bloom, *The Closing of the American Mind* (New York: Simon and Shuster, 1987), pp. 42–43, 58–67, 74–78, 118–21, 136–37, passim.

preparation and delivery of sermons or of the psychology of counseling—is to draw those theories back into the structure of the theological disciplines. Otherwise, homiletics lies in danger of becoming identical with secular rhetoric, and ministerial counseling with the psychiatrist's couch. The uniqueness of ministry, recently and very pointedly identified by John Leith as "what the church has to say that no one else can say,"[29] lies in the religious wholeness and theological unity of the task—where preaching is not merely speechmaking, and counseling offers something distinct from psychoanalysis—and in the answerability of our practice to the biblical, historical, and systematic identity of Christianity in the contemporary interpretation of its doctrines.

The unity of theological study via the examination of the biblical, historical, and systematic disciplines *as they relate* to the life of the believing community is not, therefore, a purely academic, curricular, or theoretical issue. It is an issue involving the most fundamental values in and of the practice of Christianity. The contemporary emphasis on technique and operations in ministry, like the various techniques in psychological counseling, is not problematic to the church in and of itself—it only becomes problematic when it moves toward the exclusion of biblical, historical, and systematic categories from practice, because then it has ceased to be distinctively Christian and to be the means of the communication of the values held by the church in its rich tradition.

THE WORK OF FORMULATION

All of the areas of study discussed in this chapter belong to the work of contemporary formulation and draw, whether directly or indirectly, on the materials presented in the discussion of "biblical and historical foundations" in chapter 2. This formulation consists both in word and in act—in other words, it is both systematic and practical, both theory and praxis. It is

---

[29]Cf. John H. Leith, *The Reformed Imperative: What the Church Has to Say That No One Else Can Say* (Philadelphia: Westminster, 1988).

crucial to the work of contemporary formulation—and to the unity of theology in its biblical, historical, systematic, and practical model—that we not only address the contemporary issue of theory and practice but that we enlighten and enrich our approach to this issue through some recovery of the historical understanding of the theoretical and the practical balance of theology.

Practical theology must not be left out in the cold, so to speak, understood as an activity only remotely related to the "theoretical disciplines" or as an "application" of theory without a clear mechanism by which that application can take place. For instance, we need to overcome what one of my professors called "the black box" approach to homiletical application. His point was that exegetical method typically concludes with the meaning of a text in its original historical context while homiletics typically requires, as a foundational step, some statement of the significance of the text in the present. Neither exegesis nor homiletics offers a method of moving from original meaning to contemporary significance. What is left to the exegetically responsible preacher is "the black box": the results of exegesis are thrown into one door of the box and the application of the text to the present is taken out of another door on the opposite side. One has the impression of a somewhat mysterious and arbitrary passage, of a magical act, rather than of an organic relationship between original meaning and application. What went on inside the box remains a secret, and the arbitrariness of the procedure is obscured from view by a few well-placed anecdotes.

We do not want to set aside the modern insight into practical theology as requiring an activity in the world: our praxis does not consist simply in the contemplation of a goal, however much the goal ought to be the primary focus of all Christian activity. Nonetheless, Farley is quite correct in seeing the quandary of modern theological education as arising in large part from the reduction of theology to training in "something that clergy need in order to be leaders of the church community" rather than in a particular kind of knowing "attendant on

Christian existence."[30] If there is a solution to this problem, it must arise out of a recognition of the churchly or communal character of both the words and the acts belonging to theology and, therefore, out of a recognition of the biblical-historical tradition in which those words and acts have been and continue to be generated. All words and acts belonging to the tradition, whether in its past or in its present forms, ought to be understood in the light of the redemptive goal of the church's preaching—and that goal both identifies the practical aspect of all theology (in the older sense of "practical") and demonstrates the substantial relationship of the disciplines now identified as "practical" or "ministerial" theology to the classical areas of study, the biblical, historical, and systematic disciplines.

When systematic theology in the larger sense—the contemporary discipline of theological statement—fails to take seriously the foundational materials provided by biblical and historical study, it not only brings down on itself the charge of methodological ineptitude and of failure to recognize its own historical conditionedness, it also gives itself over to increasingly arbitrary and rootless speculations. In other words, systematic theology cannot either simply repeat the doctrinal, philosophical, and phenomenological results of previous generations or argue its own case, whether doctrinally, philosophically, or phenomenologically, in the present, without reference to the foundational disciplines.

On the other hand, systematic theology cannot afford to be merely the repetition of the results of biblical theology and the history of doctrine. A systematic theology that duplicates the materials of either one of these essentially historical disciplines will fail to address the present and will appear like a relic of the past taken from a museum. Thus, works like Ringgren's *History of the Religion of Israel* or Eichrodt's *Theology of the Old Testament* are fine works on the beliefs of ancient Israel that could be consulted with profit by anyone hoping to formulate a biblically based theology in the present. If used, however, without alteration or adaptation as the basis of a

---

[30]Farley, *Theologia*, p. 130.

contemporary dogmatics, they would produce a terrible failure—not only because they lack the New Testament materials essential to any presentation of Christian teaching, but also and *primarily* because they survey the religion of an era now dead, for the sake of an accurate presentation of the beliefs of that era. Precisely because they are admirable studies of the religion and theology of ancient Israel, they cannot also supply the form for a study of the religion or theology of the present.

The problem of using an Old Testament theology or a history of Israelite religion as a contemporary dogmatics ought to be incredibly obvious—but the same problem, phrased in terms of the use of a sixteenth- or seventeenth-century, or even a nineteenth-century theological system as a contemporary dogmatics has not been nearly as obvious to ministers and to teachers of theology. Neither Schleiermacher's *Christian Faith*, nor Turretin's *Institutio theologiae elencticae* (*Institution of Polemical Theology*), nor Calvin's *Institutes of the Christian Religion*, however highly one might estimate their contribution to the history of doctrine, can serve adequately as a contemporary dogmatics or as a textbook in a class on systematic theology! The problems with which Schleiermacher wrestles are not identical with the problems of the present. The adversaries with whom Turretin and Calvin debate—like Conrad Vorstius (many readers ought to be muttering, "Who?") or Fausto Socinus, Michael Servetus, and Andreas Osiander—are no longer of any pressing importance. And some of Calvin's "adversaries," like Peter Lombard and Thomas Aquinas, have come to be viewed as allies—even of the cause of Protestant dogmatics—or at least as such close neighbors to our own teaching that they ought to be consulted rather than attacked. From the realm of historical theology, Calvin, Turretin, and Schleiermacher can provide us with important lessons in theological formulation, useful and sometimes even archetypal patterns for the formulation or refutation of a particular point; in the realm of contemporary formulation, however, we must say something beyond what they have said.

How then do we formulate systematic theology in the present? How else but as the statement of Christian doctrine written in the light of the biblical and historical materials, in consultation with collateral disciplines belonging to our contemporary "science of the Christian religion," but on the day after the end of the "history of doctrine." The issue is to use, but not duplicate an earlier formulation, to assess earlier formulations—their meaning, significance, applicability, and the comprehensibility of their language—in the light of what we know biblically, historically, philosophically, and phenomenologically about our Christianity and its context both in this culture and among the religions of the world. The point, certainly, is *not* that every minister, teacher, and missionary must become a specialist in each and every one of a rather forbidding list of religious and theological subdisciplines, but rather that each formulator of Christian teachings needs to recognize, via an introductory acquaintance with the diversified elements within the fourfold interpretive pattern of theology, what are the issues facing the contemporary formulation of her or his Christian doctrine.

Those who become dissatisfied with the credal, confessional, and systematic formulations offered by the church, on the ground that these formulations do not coincide with the results of a restrictive exegetical enterprise, must come to terms with the historical and cultural movement of the community of belief and recognize that the text of Scripture itself and the forms of doctrinal expression are mediated by and retain their significance within the ongoing community. If it is not the role of historical or contemporary systematic and practical formulations to govern the basic task of exegesis, it surely is their role to offer an interpretive context within which exegesis can speak to the present-day church. Both the interpretation of Scripture and the interpretation of the church's tradition of doctrine are necessary to contemporary formulation—the latter, if only to make clear why we state particular issues in particular ways and how we must redirect and reformulate our theological language in the present.

The study of systematic and practical theology, therefore, like the study of history, must take on an increasingly interpretive character. The exegetical and hermeneutical approach that we have learned to apply to the text of Scripture and, hopefully, to the materials of the history of the church, must also be applied to the contemporary work of formulation. Formulation in the present must, in other words, consider the movement of history, culture, and ideas between the original context of a doctrinal formulation and the present context in which that formulation must be restated or reformulated.

The formulation, today, of a doctrine of revelation cannot simply observe the standard or classical Protestant (and, from one point of view, very useful) distinctions between "natural" and "supernatural," "general" and "special" revelation. Both distinctions must be modified in the light of the increased knowledge of religion available to us since the sixteenth- and seventeenth- and eighteenth-century adoption and development of these distinctions by Protestantism, and in the light of conceptual problems caused within Christian theology since the rise of Deism and of modern science.

In addition, any formulation of the concept of revelation must come to grips with the fact that, although Scripture certainly contains a record of the revelation given to ancient Israel and to the early Christian church, it does not have *a doctrine* of revelation in the same way that it may be said to have a doctrine of God, of creation, or of redemption in Christ. Scripture, in other words, does not discuss the character of "revelation" as such. The doctrine of revelation is a product of churchly meditation on the problem of the knowledge of God, and it has, therefore, taken on many of the assumptions of fairly recent times in our history. Distinctions that we make between different kinds of revelation reflect the shifting dogmatic meditations of the church through various eras in its history, under the influence of various philosophical and scientific perspectives.

The distinction commonly made between the natural and the supernatural assumes that some events are governed entirely within the sphere of the finite by an order of law embedded within the world-order, while other events are governed primarily by divine power exerted upon nature "from above" or from without by an intelligent Other. The former events are related to the human race as part of its environment, but they are not viewed as intentional acts directed by an intelligence (or by a will) toward human beings; the latter events are also a part of the environment of human life, but they are understood as arising out of a transcendent divine intention to act, through the things of the finite order, upon human life, for good or for ill. It is clear that this distinction is historically and culturally conditioned and does not obtain at all times or at all stages in the history of religions. Prehistoric, "primitive," and prescientific cultures make no such distinction, but rather assume all of nature to be alive, sentient, and active. All "natural" events, in this view, are filled with intentionality, and no event can be conceived of as implying a divine presence that is not somehow implied in other events. The gradual increase of human control over the natural environment has led both to the rise of science and to the contraction of religion, so that, with the rise of civilization, the distinction between the natural and the super-natural also arises.

The varieties of religion from animism to polytheism and henotheism and, finally, to various forms of monotheism (including pantheism) indicate differences in the perception of the natural order over against the supernatural. Whereas animism clearly stands in the way of the distinction between natural and supernatural by understanding all things to be infused with life and spirit, polytheism fosters the distinction between natural and supernatural by identifying a finite number of finite gods who at will (i.e., not always) act upon certain parts of the environment. The eventual ordering and arrangement of the pantheon according to speculative, cosmological concerns and the consequent emergence of the idea of a high god who is the creator of the temporal order also places considerable strain on our modern distinction between the natural and the supernatural, especially insofar as the creator is not conceived to be absent from his world after the act of creation.

Thus the tradition of Judeo-Christian monotheism, with its assumption of a creation *ex nihilo* by a transcendent divine power, together with the continuing temporal involvement of that power (providence), actually militates as much against the distinction between the natural and the supernatural, as initially defined, as do the animistic and the polytheistic models just noted. Indeed, the only forms of Western theology actually conducive to the distinction are Deism, with its view of a now-absent creator who fashioned the world in such a way that it might operate according to ordained laws in his absence, and process theology, with its conception of a finite god who does not entirely control the universal natural order.

Judeo-Christian monotheism, on the grounds of its doctrines of creation, providence, and the providential *concursus* that maintains the contingent order of creation in its created being, together with the various religious and philosophical forms of pantheism and panentheism (Hinduism, Spinozism, Absolute Idealism), must, accordingly, recognize that all phenomena are at the same time natural events and divine acts. In other words, the distinction between natural and supernatural rests on an assumption, untenable in the higher religions, of an intermittent divine presence and/or divine intervention. The distinction between natural and supernatural theology, at least to the extent that it assumes the former to be a rational construction formulated apart from the divine and the latter to be a revelational construction formulated in isolation from "natural reason," must also, therefore, be rejected as untenable in a genuinely monotheistic context.

This train of thought, incidentally, shows quite clearly the problem inherent in the neoorthodox rejection of natural theology and the *analogia entis* or "analogy of being," as somehow un-Christian and out of place in the Christian attempt to formulate theology. The analogy of being, which hypothesizes a likeness in the divine handiwork to the divine Creator and allows, therefore, a discussion of God based on the natural order, does not, as alleged by neoorthodoxy, represent a prideful and mistaken human effort to ascend toward the divine. It represents an examination of the revelation of God, brought about by divine act, in the natural order—indeed, it assumes the overcoming of an absolute dichotomy between nature and so-called supernature.

The distinction between natural and supernatural theology also is untenable and, I think, fundamentally damaging to Christianity in the modern scientific context. As science more and more completely explains the phenomena of the universe, the so-called supernatural is relegated to a smaller and smaller sphere: when a thunderstorm arose in the ancient world, it might have been credited to Yahweh by Israel or to Zeus by the Greeks; when lightning struck near Erfurt in 1505, a young Luther understood it as a sign from God and cried out to St. Anne for help; when the same phenomena are experienced today in the United States, people either commend or criticize the local television station's meteorologist—with no reference at all to the divine. Typically, we pray for help with the weather only in moments of extreme difficulty when the meteorologist forecasts no relief in sight. The theological issue here is that the loss of the sense of direct "supernatural" involvement or initiative not be allowed to become a loss of the divine relationship to the "natural" order.

Theology encountered a similar problem in the seventeenth and early eighteenth century as the Ptolemaic, geocentric view of the universe was definitively replaced by the Copernican, heliocentric conception of the solar system and, ultimately, by a conception of an infinite universe. The notion, typical of (but hardly necessary to) traditional theology, of a God and a "heaven" somewhere "out there" had to be modified by a rather different notion of divine presence. If, on the one hand, by our theology and piety we maintain, unconsciously, the notion of God "out there" at the edge of the solar system while, on the other hand, we assume, again virtually unconsciously, that the supernatural is to be understood only as a rare intervention in the natural order, we will end up with a sense of the absence of God. The theory of an infinite universe demands, among other things, a stronger emphasis on divine immanence—what I would call a presence so ultimate that it could be identified as a transcendent immanence, transcending, that is, the usual understanding of immanence. Once again, the radical, Deistic distinction between natural and supernatural and, therefore, between natural and supernatural revelation, must be abandoned.

The language of natural and supernatural, general and special revelation can be maintained only when it is understood as distinguishing between an original, generalized revelation of the divine, grounded in the divine presence in and through all things, and a subsequent, special and gracious revelation of the divine, specific to a single religion, distinguishing it from all others, and understood as the completion and fulfillment of the original revelation, in and for a particular community of belief. Thus our view of revelation must take into consideration the phenomenon identified in the early part of this century by Fr. Wilhelm Schmidt as "primitive monotheism": there is a general belief in the one God or, at least, in an ultimate "high god" or creator god, held throughout the world by peoples usually identified as "primitive." Often, as in the case of the Australian Bushman, this monotheism is associated closely with a highly developed ethic not unlike the Decalogue. Such data, gathered by students of the history and phenomenology of religion, prevent us from claiming either that Christianity is just revelation and not also a religion or that the religions of the world do not have revelation. In addition, the concept of a "general revelation" ought not to be understood as defining a "natural" as opposed to a "supernatural" revelation or as indicating a revelation of truths about God so accessible to unaided reason as to be useless or inconsequential. Rather, the concept indicates a body of beliefs held in common across a large spectrum of world religion, as distinct from those beliefs held within each religion. Our theology must recognize the breadth and generality of revelation, the common elements of many religions, as well as identifying clearly the particularity of our own Christian message of salvation and the "special" or specialized revelation, held and respected within the Christian community, on which that message is founded.

These considerations of the problem of theological formulation point us back to our original question, the question of the unity of theology, of theological study, and, ultimately, of theological discourse. We ought to be prepared, however, to return to the topic on another, hopefully higher, level and to raise issues of interpretation arising out of our meditation on the historical character of Christian theology in its developing systematic and practical aspects. We ought also to be able to hold more clearly in view the issue of the relationship of patterns of study and formulation to the issue of the cultivation of the spiritual and moral values conveyed by the materials of theology, specifically with a view to understanding how the interpretation of the tradition of belief is also an exercise in the inculcation and activation of those values.

4

THE UNITY OF
THEOLOGICAL DISCOURSE

The entire argument of this book has tended toward the identification of a modified fourfold encyclopedia of theology as a useful model not only for the study and general understanding but also for the formulation of theology in the present day. The traditional breakdown of theology into the biblical, historical, systematic, and practical fields remains a useful tool, particularly when these four "fields" are recognized as parts of a historical/hermeneutical model rather than as a group of rigidly defined and easily controllable subject areas for short-term study. The "diversified encyclopedia" identified by Farley is a fact of contemporary theological life and the specialization of the various subdisciplines will not disappear. Nonetheless, a case can be made for the competent grasp at an introductory level of all or at least most of the various subdisciplines. And, more importantly, a hermeneutically unified model for understanding these subdisciplines both in their relationships to one another and in their relationship to contemporary theological formulation can be constructed.

This hermeneutical unity, moreover, was embedded in the initial construction of the fourfold model by at least some of the encyclopedists of the nineteenth century. Christoph Luthardt, writing in the mid-nineteenth century could argue that, rightly understood, the usual division into biblical, historical, systematic and practical theology is justified by the nature of the subject, inasmuch as Christianity, of which theology is the science, rests on revelation as it was handed down originally in the Holy Scripture; has a history in the church, which is the home of Christianity; gains expression in a body of doctrine, which forms a system; while the church, by means of the practical life, is carried on into the future.[1]

To state the case even more theologically, the scriptural principle of the Reformation requires an initial distinction between biblical and historical theology, while the biblical commands to believe and to obey create the distinction between the disciplines of thought and action, system and practice.

The first theological point—the scriptural principle—establishes the fourfold encyclopedia as an interpretive model over against the threefold division of study into philosophical, historical, and practical theology advocated by Schleiermacher. Schleiermacher's very compelling model was based on a series of methodological considerations that remain a part of our theological efforts in the present. According to his model, philosophy or system deals with the descriptive science of religious feeling, practical theology deals with religious doing or action, while historical theology occupies a methodological center between the present-day descriptive science of feeling and the praxis of doing by analyzing the historical course of the church's feeling and doing—and by critiquing or justifying contemporary forms by means of its analysis. This historical center consists of the study of Scripture and of the historical church, inasmuch as the historical method applies to both areas of study.

Emphasis on the scriptural principle maintains a theological distinction between Scripture and the tradition of the historical church, between the prior biblical norm of Christian teaching and the secondary, pedagogical, and interpretive norm of the church's tradition. It also places the study of Scripture

---

[1]Christoph Luthardt, *Kompendium der Dogmatik*, 11th posthumous ed. (Leipzig: Dörffling & Franke, 1914), §4.1.

and, in a certain sense, the study of the tradition, prior to the formulation of theological system in the present. From a methodological and hermeneutical point of view, the historical approach characteristic of both biblical and church-historical studies becomes the rule for understanding the fundamental issues at stake in doctrinal theology. The second theological point drawn from Luthardt—the distinction between systematic and practical—accords with the rest of Schleiermacher's argument.

The logic of the fourfold definition of theology can also be stated in a more philosophical form, as evidenced by the arguments in Julius Räbiger's *Encyclopedia of Theology* (1879). Räbiger's work manifests the influences of idealist philosophy and assumes, in Hegelian fashion, that Christianity is the absolute religion and, as such, the highest manifestation of the phenomenon of religion. The objection to the fourfold model of the study of theology, that it follows the pattern of a historical development and is therefore accidental and unnecessary, he argues, fails to consider the integral relationship between the historical reality of Christianity and the historical character of the study of Christianity. "If theology has the task of attaining to a knowledge of Christianity, viewed in its connection with the historical religions, according to its historical reality, . . . [theology] must also ground its principle of arrangement upon the historical course of Christianity."[2]

We must regard Christ, Räbiger continues, as the founder of Christianity and, consequently, the truth revealed in Christ as the underlying truth that makes possible the life of the church. The church is, therefore, the "organ" that gives historical expression to the truth of Christ. This relationship between Christ and the church points toward four stages in the development of Christianity and four basic divisions of the task of study: the "origin," the "historical development," the

---

[2]Julius F. Räbiger, *Encyclopaedia of Theology*, trans. John Macpherson, 2 vols. (Edinburgh: T. & T. Clark, 1884), 1:297.

"Christian spirit . . . becoming the subject of ideal treatment," and the movement toward "practical application."[3]

Without accepting the philosophy underlying Räbiger's remarks about the spiritual necessity of the development of religion toward the absolute, it is quite possible to see in his analysis, as in Luthardt's, a proper grasp of the historical character of the science of religion and an equally accurate view of the interpretive structure given to Christianity by its history and, therefore, capable of analysis in a contemporary interpretive science of the Christian religion. The unity of theological study is an interpretive unity resting on a historical trajectory of belief and a historical approach to the materials of belief as they reflect the thought and the action of the believing community. This unity, moreover, can be described in terms of the objective discipline of study and analysis as well as the subjective involvement of the individual in the life of the community. The task of this final chapter is to present an overview of this unity.

OBJECTIVITY AND SUBJECTIVITY

Theology has never been a purely academic discipline. The phenomenon of an academic study of religion and of teachers of theology who are responsible only (or at least primarily) to educational institutions is a comparatively recent one. The fathers of the church and the theologians of the early Middle Ages were all churchmen—bishops, priests, monks—involved in the preaching of the gospel and in the daily work of organizing and administering the life of the church. Their writings are, for the most part, occasional: Augustine did not write on baptism, the church, and predestination simply for the sake of producing up-to-date theological formulae; rather, his treatises on these subjects arose directly out of debate over the nature and content of the church's teaching. Even Augustine's great treatise *On the Trinity* arose out of religious need, in part out of a churchly desire to clarify an important issue for the faithful, in part our of a desire to provide a definitive treatise

---

[3]Ibid., p. 299.

against the continuing Arian threat in the West, and in part out of a personal spiritual concern to meditate on this most profound of theological topics. Similarly, Gregory the Great's *Pastoral Rule* arose directly out of the writer's own experience of governance in the church and was intended as a guide to others who followed the same path as Gregory toward the office of bishop.

This daily involvement of theologians in the life of the church did not cease with the rise of the monastic schools and universities in the twelfth century. We might be led to expect that the creation of schools and of academic specialists, professors of theology, to teach in the universities would lead to a separation of theological study from churchly concerns and from personal piety, but such was not the case. One of the most philosophically significant essays of the early scholastic era, Anselm's *Proslogion*, found its point of origin in the spiritual life of the monastery and took the form of a prayer. Its author lived out his life as an active abbot and an archbishop involved in the debates over the extent of royal power to invest bishops. Major systematizers of theology such as Bonaventure, Albert the Great, and Thomas Aquinas served as vicars of their orders, bishops, and defenders of the faith who saw their theology as an integral part of the religious life. In the eras of the Reformation and post-Reformation orthodoxy the theologians who did not also occupy pulpits were the exceptions, not the rule.

The study of theology, then, throughout the greater part of the Christian tradition, was a study of materials relevant to the life of the church and to the spirituality of the individual. More than this, meditation on the materials of theology was a spiritual as well as an academic discipline. The discipline of theology—indeed, the discipline of studying theology—ought to create in the mind of the student a series of patterns of ideas and interpretations that can frame and influence both mind and will, thought and action. Thus the unity of theological study and of theological curriculum or theological formulation must not be a unity only of objectively stated ideas that cohere in a systematic form, but also a unity, subjectively experienced, of thought and action. The creation of a cohesive systematization of Christian doctrine will not be sufficient by itself to the creation of a unified and fruitful pattern of study. Nor, on the other hand, will the cultivation of piety or spirituality be successful apart from a well-conceived program of study in the so-called theoretical or academic subdisciplines of theology. Theological study, in order to maintain, or shall we say, regain, the crucial role that it has played throughout the earlier history of the church, will have to balance once again the theoretical and the practical, the objective and the subjective elements of the religious life.

Another clue to the unity of the discipline can be found in the patristic practice of citing Scripture. Beginning students of patristics are frequently surprised and a bit befuddled by the mixture of precise and seemingly imprecise citations of Scripture with what appear to be allusions or even virtual quotations that appear without citation in the text. Are the church fathers guilty of a form of sloppy referencing that would be unacceptable today in a student paper? No, not at all. On the one hand, it is certainly true that the modern style of precise documentation has been in use for only a few hundred years. On the other hand, and far more importantly, the church fathers were less interested in citing Scripture than in thinking biblically and traditionally. Their patterns of citation and of interpretation were quite like the patterns found in Scripture itself, granting, however, that they had a sense of the distinction between their own writings and those of either the Old Testament or the apostolic authors.

There were, of course, no quotation marks in the original writings of the fathers. Modern editors have identified the quotations and have given them the chapter and verse references that exist only in modern (post–fifteenth-century) editions of Scripture. The fathers themselves evidence an approach to the text of Scripture that ranges across a spectrum of usage from precise quotation to less precise referencing, to paraphrase, to increasingly vague allusion—probably in most cases resting on memory rather than on a codex of the Old Testament or New Testament immediately at hand. Again, their purpose was not precise quotation but rather biblical or biblical-traditional thinking and speaking: the words of the text become their words, the thoughts expressed or implied by the text their thoughts, with the result that the patristic writings offer a theological tapestry through which threads from Scripture, threads from the tradition, and threads from the mind of the author are woven into a more or less harmonious whole.

What the writers of the patristic period manifest so clearly, then, is a unity of theological thinking—and of Christian living—that arises out of a total immersion of an author in Scripture, in tradition, and in the church's life of the present. Scripture has meaning in the writer's present because he is immersed in a tradition of reading and understanding the text that mediates the text to him and that ratifies its meaning and usefulness to the present. What is more, this sense of the meaning and usefulness of the biblical witness moves on both the doctrinal and the practical levels. The patristic writers do not separate doctrine from spirituality and spirituality from the daily life of the Christian community.

Several other clues to the success of writers of past ages in their efforts to integrate theological study in and with the life of the church can be found in the basic definitions of theology that come to us from the classic formulations of both the Catholic and Protestant traditions. I refer to the great theological syntheses of the medieval doctors and the Protestant orthodox theologians. These churchly teachers recognized that theology must indicate, objectively, a recognizable body of teaching and, subjectively, an inward disposition to know it.

Theology, objectively considered, is an academic discipline. It claims a distinct body of knowledge as its own or, when aspects or elements of that body of knowledge also belong to other disciplines, it claims a distinct approach and rationale for dealing with that knowledge. In the language of past centuries, theology is called a *scientia* or "science." Both the term *scientia* and the understanding of the theological task have, as we have seen, altered substantially since theology was first called a science by Alain of Lille and his contemporaries in the late twelfth century. The term, however, is still applied to theology and, more importantly, is capable, when rightly interpreted, of providing theological study with a sense of method and direction. It is, after all, one thing to call theology an academic discipline and quite another to call it a science, particularly granting the connotations of present-day English usage. The former description is rather loose and could be applied to virtually any subject that is taught in schools, colleges, universities, and seminaries. Since theology has a history, has documents and materials drawn from that history, and has contemporary expositors, it most certainly can be taught—if only from the point of view of history. But the fact that it can be turned into an academic discipline and taught does not demonstrate anything concerning the character and quality of its materials and claims. Heresies can be taught; the materials and theories of discredited philosophies can be gathered and examined in a classroom; the most arbitrary and outrageous theosophy can be the object of academic investigation as long as it is documented; and outmoded worldviews can be examined out of historical interest. The academic investigation may be legitimate while the subject-matter being investigated may be fraudulent or worthless, or simply inapplicable to the concerns of the present.

The latter description, the identification of theology as a science, however, implies that theology is a cogent discipline, a legitimate subject for study in its own right. Both in the twelfth century and in the twentieth, the description of theology as a science forces the discipline of theology to examine not only its materials but also the character and quality of its materials and of their claims. When theology was first called a science, the term *scientia* meant a distinct body of knowledge that contained its own self-evident first principles together with the conclusions that could be drawn from them—in other words, an independent, self-sustaining intellectual discipline resting on legitimate presuppositions and possessing its own internal logic and coherence.

This identification of theology as a unified *scientia* was considerably easier to maintain prior to the eighteenth century than it is today. The problem of the "diversified encyclopedia" and of the specialization of the academic practitioners of each subdiscipline give one the impression that if theology can be called a "science" in any sense, it ought to be defined as a grouping of more or less related sciences than as a single science. In addition, the critique of rational metaphysics leveled by Kant at the end of the eighteenth century and the reconstruction of theology proposed by Schleiermacher at the beginning of the nineteenth have led many theologians away from all definitions of theology that focus on it as a form of knowledge: it is either an ethical system (a ground for doing) or an experiential system (a description of profound feeling). In either case, it cannot be a *scientia* in any sense of the term.

Beyond this, it has been precisely the more "scientific" or critical aspects of modern theological reflection that have typically been seen as barriers or even threats to the large-scale systematization of theology—or even to the establishment of a unifying structure for understanding the theology of the Old Testament or of the New. Post-Enlightenment exegesis has forced theology to ask critical scientific and textual questions that frequently render the path to traditional theological formulation difficult if not impossible. Inasmuch as most of the formulae and doctrinal expositions of the older dogmatics draw on a tradition of exegesis that is no longer directly accessible to us—particularly in view of its typological and allegorical aspects and its tendency to move away from rather than toward the grammatical meaning of a text in its original life-situation. The hermeneutical gap between the text and the dogmas and between the dogmas and the contemporary situation calls into question our ability to construct a "science of theology" out of these very diverse and divergent materials.

Finally, the contemporary mind discerns such differences in approach between disciplines commonly called sciences— chemistry, physics, and biology, or, granting the presence of social sciences, anthropology and sociology—and theology that the name "science" appears hardly to fit the theological disciplines. The intensity of the problem can be seen in a theological work like Charles Hodge's famous *Systematic Theology*. There we see an effort to understand theology as a science in the context of the highly empirical mood of late nineteenth-century chemistry, physics, and geology. Hodge argues that Scripture, like the earth, provides raw data in an unordered manner—and that theology, like geology, performs an inductive analysis of the data that discerns the order and draws sound conclusions leading to a systematic presentation. The fundamental flaw in heterodox theologies, Hodge argued, was an imperfect induction from the basic evidence.[4]

The impossibility of maintaining such a perspective ought to be obvious. The claim of physics that, at a constant temperature, the volume of a given quantity of gas is inversely proportionate to the pressure—Boyle's law—has a rather different cognitive status than the claim of theology that "God so loved the world that he gave his one and only Son, that whoever believes in him shall not perish but have eternal life" (John 3:16). The grammar used in physical and spiritual propositions may well be structurally equivalent, but the subject-matter is so vastly different that the two sets of truths belong to qualitatively different realms of discourse: the constancy of temperature, the quantity of gas, and the degree of pressure are all measurable, verifiable terms—God's love, the divine sonship of Jesus of Nazareth, perdition, and everlasting life are neither measurable nor verifiable, at least not according to the same criteria. All of the terms of Boyle's law represent physically demonstrable and repeatable data, whereas none of the terms in John 3:16 are physical, demonstrable, or in any way repeatable. Also, the logic of Hodge's argument, if pressed to its own conclusions, would make systematic theology, as written by Hodge, a more desirable and perhaps superior form of knowledge than Scripture itself (granting that geology and physics are superior to unorganized perceptions of the natural order)—a conclusion that Hodge himself would surely have wished to avoid. If theology is a science, it will have to be defined as one neither in terms of the old scholastic definition nor in terms like those adopted by Hodge from the physical sciences.

---

[4]Charles Hodge, *Systematic Theology*, 3 vols. (1871–73; repr. Grand Rapids: Eerdmans, 1975), 1:1–2.

Significantly, Hodge disagreed with his textbook and model, Francis Turretin's *Institutio theologiae* on this point: Turretin had argued explicitly that theology is not a science because it is not based on rational evidence but rather on teachings to be accepted by faith.[5] What Turretin recognized—and, indeed, what most of the older dogmaticians, including those who did define theology as a science also understood—was that the materials offered in Scripture were fundamentally different from those offered by nature for inductive analysis or, for that matter, by reason alone for purely deductive construction. From the vantage point of the present, we can clearly see that Hodge's approach to theology as a science analogous to geology falls into the same predicament as the so-called biblical-theology movement of this century did in its language of "the God who acts in history": the religious "data" presented by Scripture is, already in the form it takes in the text itself, the subject of theological interpretation. A "mighty act of God," like the Israelite crossing of the Red Sea, was not interpreted as such by the Egyptians and, if it could be re-viewed by a neutral "scientific" observer—a meteorologist, for example—of the twentieth century, it could just as easily be explained on purely natural grounds. The point is not that the religious explanation needs to be set aside but only that it represents, in itself, a step beyond mere "data" and that its use in theology places theology outside of the realm of empirical science.[6]

The problem here is not merely one of nomenclature. Theology claims to deal, both objectively and subjectively, with a distinct body of knowledge and with knowledge generally from a distinct perspective. Even if the definition of theology as a science, used here as a convenient starting point for discussion, is set aside, the problem remains. In the twentieth century there are major barriers to the identification

---

[5]Francis Turretin, *Institutio theologiae elencticae*, 3 vols. (Geneva, 1677–89; reissued, Edinburgh and New York, 1847), I.vi.5.

[6]Cf. Vern S. Poythress, *Symphonic Theology* (Grand Rapids: Zondervan, 1987), p. 49 for a theological perspective on the inseparability of event and interpretation.

of theology as a methodologically unified discipline dealing with a cohesive body of knowledge. These barriers need to be surmounted if theology is to remain—or, some might say, become again—both a substantive and a useful study.

Somewhat more difficult to argue is the objective character of theological formulation over against the Kantian and Schleiermacherian critiques and in the light of postcritical exegesis. Kant argued that our categories of perception and understanding are categories of mind that interpret and frame our experience of phenomena. By extension of this argument, "things-in-themselves," or noumena, that lie behind the phenomena of our experience are not the source of the interpretive categories—such as quantity, quality, space, time, and cause. Kant's conclusion was that reason could not reach these things-in-themselves and that rational metaphysics, which assumed that space, time, and cause were in things and could be used in arguments for the existence of God, was a fallacy. According to Kant, the content of religion was not rational knowledge of a divine noumenon but rather an ethics based on subjectively rooted moral values and directed toward the divine as the guarantor of those values. In this Kantian perspective, the objective basis for dogmas is lost.[7]

Schleiermacher's explanation of the contents of dogmatics as a series of objectifications of the feeling of absolute or utter dependence was an attempt to reconstruct theology following the Kantian critique of rational knowing. If indeed God is an unknowable noumenon, then even our theology cannot "know" God, but we can encounter the divine reality at a deeper level, the level of "feeling," or, as Schleiermacher's term might be translated, with greater justice, "immediate apprehension." Thus Schleiermacher endeavored to set theology on a different foundation, a foundation not subject to the Kantian critique of rational metaphysics. Theologians in the nineteenth

---

[7]Cf. Royce G. Gruenler, *Meaning and Understanding: The Philosophical Framework for Biblical Interpretation*, Foundations of Contemporary Interpretation, vol. 4 (Grand Rapids: Zondervan, 1990) for a review of the history of philosophy as it bears on epistemological issues.

century soon realized, however, that this deobjectification of the ground of theology was not entirely satisfactory: if all dogmas are but reflections on a single kind of consciousness, the question remains concerning the correlation between these objectifications and the identity of the being on whom we are absolutely dependent. In other words, if dogmas are objectifications of feeling, and if this feeling arises out of an encounter with and a consciousness or immediate apprehension of a reality noumenal or otherwise, then the dogmas must have some reference to that reality. The question of objectivity returns and demands an answer. Ludwig Feuerbach, in a sense, stood Schleiermacher on his head by arguing that the language of theology was only a projection of the subjective hopes and desires of human beings. The so-called Mediating School moved theology in the other direction, retaining some of Schleiermacher's emphasis on consciousness, particularly on the self-consciousness of Jesus, and sought to find, in the historical Jesus, a basis for objective theological statement: we are thrown back, even after Kant, on the sense of theology as a discipline with an objective content, but also with a subjective or personal reference.

If not entirely satisfactory as a statement of the objectivity of theology, Schleiermacher's theology did serve to direct attention both theologically and hermeneutically to the subjective aspects of theology—both to the individual and to the corporate experience of belief. His work is particularly important, even to the more conservative side of Christianity, because he recognized so clearly that the personal, subjective basis of theology is mediated in and through the community of belief and that doctrines and practices become important to individuals and the conduct of individuals is modified by structures of belief in and through the life of the corporate community of faith.

Granting this insight, we are able to argue that the subjective side of theology, defined by the older orthodoxy as a habit or disposition of knowing (*habitus sciendi*), arises in an individual in community and that the ongoing historical life of the community is necessary to the mediation of objective statements of doctrine, as significant statements, to individuals. In other words, we recognize the interrelationship, in theology and religion, of the objective and objectivizing statement of doctrine with the individual formulator and of both the doctrine itself and the formulator with the ongoing life of the community of faith. Theology arises and becomes significant in this corporate context of belief and interpretation.

The subjectivity of belief and interpretation, whether considered as thought or as action, is not the subjectivity of the isolated ego. Piety and spirituality are developed in and through the interaction of believers with one another in the context of an ongoing, living tradition of faith and obedience. Insofar as the formal study of theology takes place within this ongoing community of belief, moreover, the objectivity sought under the rubric of theology as "science" and the subjectivity identified under the rubric of theology as "disposition" complement one another.

Indeed, what goes on at a spiritual level in the study of theology very closely resembles the contemplative exercise described by Tilden Edwards as "re-membering"—an escape from the isolation of our own limited temporality through the use of memory in meditation. Memory, he notes, "affects all the other dimensions" of our lives "through the imprints of experience it carries into the present." Even so, it is through the opening of memory to the religious dimension that self-healing can take place and, in the presence of the larger reality, "God, self, and world are re-membered."[8] Theological study should serve to open the individual spirit to the spiritual life of the community in such a way that the many-faceted spirituality of the tradition enriches the spirituality of the individual, drawing and developing it beyond its own limited resources. The corporate memory of the community becomes the possession of the individual memory—not totally, of course, but in such measure that the corporate testimony enriches and interprets the individual's language of faith.

---

[8]Tilden Edwards, *Living in the Presence: Disciplines for the Spiritual Heart* (San Francisco: Harper & Row, 1987), pp. 77, 85, 96.

This necessary interrelationship of the objective and the subjective ought not to stand in the way of theology, rightly understood as the "science of the Christian religion." Scientific theory, in the "exact sciences" as well as in the human and social sciences, has long since set aside the illusion of "detached objectivity" in scientific inquiry. The scientist is not a neutral observer who has no involvement with her work. Not only must a scientist have an initial reason for doing the work and a commitment to the completion of the investigation arising out of interest, but also the observer's or investigator's own patterns and categories of knowing belong both to the work of observation and to the work of interpretation. In other words, the scientist is and must be involved in the identification of data, in the selection of significant data, and in the interpretation of the data and its significance. In fact, there is arguably a prejudgment concerning significance in the initial identification and selection of data.

A similar point can be made concerning historical study. Historians recognize that there is no such thing as a "brute fact." "Facts" or, as they are better termed, "data" or "traces," are preserved, are selected, and are interpreted because someone or some group has identified them as significant either by creating traces of such a nature that they will remain intact or by selecting certain data rather than other data for interpretation. Even the collection and publication of documents without comment or analysis is an act of interpretation, granting that some selection and some judgment concerning significance has been made. Involvement with and commitment to the materials of history does not in itself indicate loss of the objective or scientific nature of the inquiry.

By extension, and in view of the historical methods used in the investigation, involvement in the religious does not bar an individual from the scientific study of religion.[9] In fact, some

---

[9]On the nature of historical objectivity, see Marc Bloch, *The Historian's Craft* (New York: Vintage, 1953); E. H. Carr, *What Is History?* (New York: Vintage, 1963); G. J. Renier, *History: Its Purpose and Method* (New York: Harper & Row, 1950), and Trygve Tholfsen, *Historical Thinking: An Introduction* (New York:

level of involvement is necessary in the initial selection of the study of religion as opposed to some other study.

HERMENEUTICAL CIRCLES

The unity of the theological task—in fact, the ability to engage productively in the theological task—rests on the intimate and meaningful relationship of the tradition found within the canon of Scripture and the tradition of interpretation, theology, and spirituality, to the believing community of the present and to the individual interpreter as part of that community. Standing in the way of such a relationship is the relative isolation of a dogmatically defined and exposited canon of Scripture from the history of Christian theology and spirituality, from the patterns and practices of contemporary critical exegesis, and of both of these ingredients of theology from the present-day life of the church.

The reason that Scripture is authoritative—apart from our traditional doctrinal statements concerning its divine inspiration and its authority as a doctrinal norm—is that its contents are mirrored in the life of the church and that, in this historical process of reflection, the believing community has gradually identified as canon the books that rightly guide and reflect its faith while setting aside those books that fail to reflect its faith adequately. The history of Christian theology and spirituality has not only carried this canon forward and delivered it to the present day; it has also provided an ongoing meditation on the contents of the canon in relation to the life of the church. This meditation, in turn, has assured contemporary recognition of the continuing relevance of the biblical message to the believing community. There is, in other words, a necessary interrelationship between all questions of theological formulation and the

---

Harper & Row, 1967). On the problem of objectivity in the application of historical materials to theological formulation, see further, Richard A. Muller, "The Role of Church History in the Study of Systematic Theology," in *Doing Theology in Today's World*, ed. Thomas McComiskey and John Woodbridge (Grand Rapids: Zondervan, 1990), chapter 4.

ongoing interpretive life of the church. The movement from the authoritative text to the formulation of doctrine as accomplished in the life of the believing community is necessarily circular.

At the heart of the enormous churchly, curricular, and systematic problem that presently confronts theology is the issue of hermeneutics. Of all of the issues noted in the preceding chapters, the issue of hermeneutics is arguably the most pressing, because it is the most fundamental. And its settlement is arguably the only basis for a convincing solution to the other problems. Establishment of a formal and functional unity to theology in its several disciplines cannot be a matter of artificial or external construction. Rather, it must be a theological task internal to the disciplines themselves in their relationships, a task that is essentially interpretive in nature.

One way to approach this hermeneutical or interpretive task is to ask the question of how and why a text—any text, whether biblical, church historical, or contemporary—comes to us with an identifiable meaning that is grounded in its original intentions and original historical, cultural, religious, and social milieu, how and why that meaning can be known by us, how and why that meaning, as preserved through a long history or mediated by contemporary events, yields up a significance for us in our own situation. The answer to such questions is often given in terms of the construction or identification of a "hermeneutical circle."

The concept of a "hermeneutical circle" comes to us from the nineteenth century, most probably from the work of Friedrich Ast (1778-1841), one of the first writers to sketch out the foundations for the modern science of interpretation or hermeneutics. The idea was subsequently developed at length by Friedrich Schleiermacher (1768-1834) and has since become the common property of virtually all students of interpretation and of the theory of interpretation.[10] The basic idea of the

---

[10]Cf. Richard E. Palmer, *Hermeneutics: Interpretation Theory in Schleiermacher, Dilthey, Heidegger, and Gadamer* (Evanston: Northwestern University Press, 1969), pp. 76–81, 87–88.

hermeneutical circle arises from the recognition that there is more to understanding a text than the parsing of its various clauses or phrases. The meaning of the parts belongs to the whole—and the whole, the larger frame of reference of the text, is larger than the text itself. The hermeneutical circle indicates the whole and its parts, the understanding of the parts with reference to the whole and of the whole with reference to its parts—and, specifically, the understanding of a single part with reference to the other parts and to the whole to which it belongs.

What is most important about this idea of a hermeneutical circle is that it recognizes the intimate involvement of the interpreter with the work of interpretation. The circle has, of course, an objective rootage in the verbal meaning of a text (the part) and in the larger significance (the whole) of the document as placed into its proper intellectual, cultural, and religious context—but the circle is, primarily, a description of the way in which the mind of the interpreter ought to approach the document, i.e., with a view to understanding the part in relation to the whole and the whole in relation to the part. As a preliminary inquiry we must, therefore, ask about the nature of the circle: How can the legitimate circle arise—i.e., what is the nature of the relationship of the interpreter to the text that gives rise to a legitimate and truly fruitful circle of understanding, that knows the part and the whole in relation to one another—and what or *where*, precisely, is this mysterious "whole" that guides our interpretation of the textual part? Hirsch notes, importantly, that this whole can be identified, at least in a preliminary manner, in terms of questions concerning the genre of the document.[11]

Identification of genre is a fundamental interpretive step in all disciplines. In theology, we tend to identify such questions with biblical exegesis—particularly with so-called form criticism. But the question is of much broader application. It belongs not only to biblical studies but also to historical and

---

[11]E. D. Hirsch, *Validity in Interpretation* (New Haven: Yale University Press, 1967), pp. 76–77.

systematic theology, and it even has an application in the practical or ministerial field. In historical studies, as in biblical, the identification of genre consists, typically, in the initial characterization of a document as to kind and in the subsequent recognition of the limitation placed on its scope and contents by its basic intentionality or purpose. More than simply an identification of the "kind" of document, the answer to the question of genre provides an opening into the mind of the author and the function of the document for the interpreter—it is, in a sense, the point of entry into the hermeneutical circle or, from the vantage of the interpreter, the moment of the preliminary and tentative creation of the circle.

In the systematic and practical fields, this basic question is also present, but not always or even primarily with reference to a historical document. There are, of course, moments of study in which students, pastors, and teachers take up a document written in the field of systematic or practical theology and—if they wish to enter the thought-world of its author and learn from the document—ask the question of genre. One does not approach a book on pastoral counseling as a first level of preparation for a sermon or a system of theology for help in pastoral counseling. On a far deeper level, the level of individual formulation and preparation, however, the hermeneutical question of genre presents itself in systematic and practical theology in the form of an identification of task. As I will argue further, below, this identification of task, understood as a hermeneutical venture, takes on meaning and depth in relation to the individual interpreter's ability to enter into and draw on the historical life of the believing community in the creation of a living "hermeneutical circle" in contemporary formulation.

To return to our three basic questions concerning the nature and character of the circle: How can the legitimate circle arise—i.e., what is the nature of the relationship of the interpreter to the text that gives rise to a legitimate and truly fruitful circle of understanding, that knows the part and the whole in relation to one another—and what or *where*, precisely, is this mysterious "whole" that guides our interpretation of the textual part?

Everything I have just said about the hermeneutical circle assumes the text (or the task) and the exegete/interpreter or theologian. I do not want to leave the impression, as is sometimes done in contemporary manuals of hermeneutics and biblical interpretation, that interpretation occurs between the text and the exegete in a manner exclusive of any other parties to the exchange or task: the exegete, armed with a set of lexical and grammatical tools, aided perhaps by a commentary or two and by a broad acquaintance with the history and culture of the age in which the text was written, engineers a frontal assault on the text. Out of the literal, verbal, grammatical meaning of the words, granting their place in the whole of the book or treatise in which they occur, the implications of the text are derived. As a part of this task, the interpreter infers from the text the context or life-situation of the writer of the text, inferring problems, adversaries, or even dialogue partners implied by the text. The text and, we may hope, the document of which it is a part, can then be understood in terms of the historical, social, and cultural background of the text in which it originally spoke and found its purpose.

The "whole" that gives meaning to the part has already been identified, in these basic hermeneutical and exegetical procedures, as being larger than the document in which the text appears: it is the whole historical, cultural, and social context of the document with particular reference to the issues that gave rise to the document. The circularity as well as the importance of the procedure is obvious—if not the entirety of the historical, cultural, and social context, surely the issues that gave rise to the document have been identified by critical examination of the document itself. The larger context, however, governs the identification of issues within the purview of the document and its author: no matter how much we would like to do so, we are prevented by a right (even if necessarily incomplete) iden-tification of the context of a document from imposing our own views on it. We are prevented, for example, by our knowledge of the larger context of the gospel of Matthew from identifying the *ecclesia* that Christ founds upon the Petrine rock as—either in the mind of Christ or in the mind of the author of the Gospel—consisting in an elaborate hierarchy of deacons, priests, bishops, and pope or, alternatively, of deacons, elders (ruling and teaching), sessions, presbyteries, synods, and general assemblies! The *ecclesia* that Matthew had in mind simply did not look like the twentieth-century church.

Our ability to identify this Matthean *ecclesia*, then, rests on two basic sets of data. On the one hand, we rely on the text of the Matthew's gospel itself and, on the other, we rely on other documents from the same period of time, particularly documents from the early church that offer somewhat different perceptions of the identity of the *ecclesia*. If all we possessed were our own wits and the gospel of Matthew, we would have very little chance of developing a picture of the particular community out of which the gospel of Matthew arose, of the larger context of earliest Christianity in its cultural setting, and therefore of the limits of meaning placed by these several contexts on the term *ecclesia*. The naked hermeneutical circle of the individual exegete and the text is a hopeless circle inasmuch as neither the text nor the exegete can supply a clear picture of the larger whole of which the text is a part—not only of the pericope, but also of the entire document.

We must readily admit, then, that the hermeneutical circle is larger than the mental world of the lonely exegete confronting the isolated text. To describe the circle in this way is to threaten its legitimacy by placing it under a set of restrictions that stand in the way of interpretation. This is not merely a technical problem: such barriers are ultimately more threatening to the exegetical work of the nonspecialist, who may not fully understand the problem and who may assume—as the evidence of all too many textual or "expository" sermons indicates—that the individual and the text are all that is needed for a valid and theologically productive reading of Scripture.

Context is more than what we can infer from a text or document. The interpreter of a text must rely on broader historical, cultural, and social study and must be illuminated by archaeological discoveries and by the study of the folkways of

Israel's and the church's neighbors in the ancient world. This compares with the work of the interpreter of a text from Luther's writings who ought not simply to infer the context from a particular document but ought rather to deal with the text out of an awareness of the movement of Western thought through the later Middle Ages into the sixteenth century, of the cultural and political situation in Europe and in Saxony, and of the issues raised by the juxtaposition of the Augustinianism of Luther's monastic order with the Semi-Pelagianism of Luther's nominalist teachers at Erfurt.

In both of the cases just noted, examination of the larger context begins to answer not only the question of the "whole" and, specifically, of the genre of the document, but also the question of the significance that looms behind the deciphering of the verbal meaning of the passage. The difficulty of mastering all of these materials and of relating the materials to the text, together with the difficulty of understanding precisely what kind of approach is required by a particular document, raises for us the issue of critical method. By what right and according to what warrants do we address a text or a document and elicit meaning from it?

Surely we address any text or any document by right of our own existence, together with its existence within our present and within the admittedly vast realm of human consciousness. I believe that Aristotle was utterly correct—granting a few notable exceptions among the students I have encountered—when he announced as a basic rationale for his *Metaphysics* that "all people, by nature, desire to know." When we encounter an unknown standing in some vague relation to us, we cannot be content with calling it an "unknown." Immediately it becomes a puzzle to be solved. We see precisely this issue at stake in the problem of the "UFO," the "Unidentified Flying Object": the problem is not that there are UFOs—the problem is that these unknowns immediately become puzzles and that people persist in *identifying* them, almost invariably with bizarre results.

Just as the meaning of a particular text is hedged about and defined by the larger context out of which the text arises, so is the role of any interpreter is hedged about and defined by a context of rules and methods of interpretation. The misidentification of UFOs arises out of a certain lack of restraint on the part of the interpreter of the evidence. In fact, it arises out of a methodological error that permits the placement of real evidence into a context created by the highly imaginative authors of science fiction. In order for any legitimate interpretation to occur, there must not only be a document or some sort of evidence to be placed into a context of meaning, and an interpreter ready to perform the exegetical exercise—there must also be a set of constraints placed on the interpreter. There is a hermeneutical circle, in other words, that arises out of the interaction of the individual exegete with a text in and through the use of critical, historical method.

On the most basic level, the interpreter must have linguistic control, characterized both by a knowledge of the language in which the text is written and by a knowledge of semantics, of the way in which language works to convey meaning. Not only grammar and syntax but also figures of speech must be understood, and, in addition, an interpreter must be sensitive to the range of meaning of words and how usage governs which portion of a given range of meaning belongs to a word in a particular instance. For example, just because the Hebrew word *emet*, usually translated "truth," includes in its root the connotation of "faithfulness" or even "faithfulness in relationship" and carries that root meaning with it into certain usages, we cannot assume that "faithfulness" is part of its meaning in all contexts. Nor, when Jewish authors of the Greek New Testament use the word *aletheia*, truth, are we permitted to assume that their Jewish or Hebraic background implies *emet* under the *aletheia* and, therefore, a "Hebrew" notion of "faithfulness" somehow now attached to a Greek word that never before had such a connotation and that cannot, from its use in the Greek New Testament, be directly inferred to have that connotation.[12]

---

[12]Cf. James Barr, *The Semantics of Biblical Language* (Oxford: Oxford University Press, 1961).

When applied theologically, this "root fallacy" can have far-reaching and highly problematic results. In the case of the relationship of *aletheia* to *emet*, the conclusion has frequently been drawn that a "Greek" notion of truth as clarification of an idea or datum, often understood in a propositional sense as the right statement of a case, could not be found in Scripture. Even in the Greek text of the New Testament, it was asserted, the Greek word *aletheia* ought to be interpreted as *emet* and *emet* interpreted as a relational faithfulness, indeed, as "encounter" with a "person" rather than as the statement of a propositional truth. The problem here is that even in the Old Testament, where we are dealing with *emet*, we find a large number of cases, such as those occurring in the Book of Proverbs, in which the word is used to indicate right correspondence, clear and accurate statement, and so forth. In the Greek of the New Testament as well, the meaning of the word is determined by its linguistic context and use, not by theorizations about roots. There is no linguistic reason on earth to claim that Christ's statement to the Father "Your word is truth" (John 17:17) ought to be interpreted as "Your word is a personal encounter." Right interpretation, in this instance, has enormous implications for the theological task—for the identification of what theology is and of what theology is capable of saying about God and God's work.

The older grammatical-historical criticism and the more recent methodological tools of source, form, redaction, rhetorical, and canon criticism also provide necessary limits and restraints for interpretation. Each of these critical approaches supplements the others and provides some checks on them, hedging and defining the interpretive task and providing the interpreter with patterns and methods that can open a text. The critical tools provide a certain degree of objectivity and distance, enabling the exegete to ask questions of the text that might not normally be asked apart from the application of a clearly defined method. Thus the question of form—the genre question on a small scale—can be applied to a psalm: Is it an imprecatory psalm or a psalm of praise? The answer to the question both reveals and limits the way in which the text can be interpreted.

The value of source and redaction criticism, together with the breadth of their application to documents throughout the history of theology, can easily be seen in the case of the *Didache* or *Teaching of the Twelve Apostles*, a document of the early church recovered in 1873. The original of the document is in Greek, and the document appears to consist of two parts, an initial catechetical section describing the "two ways"—the way of good and the way of evil—and demanding that the choice for the good be made in and through Christ, and a subsequent liturgical section describing early Christian practice, including our earliest extant description of the modes of baptism. The document is of utmost importance to our understanding of the early church not only because of its late first- or early second-century date but also because of its detail concerning the kinds of ministry in at least one community and geographical area. The discussion of baptism is particularly significant inasmuch as it allows either immersion or infusion—casting some doubt on the usefulness of modern debate.

We also have in our possession a Latin version of part of the treatise, dating from a later period, and a vast elaboration of the treatise in the third-century liturgical document known as the *Constitutions of the Twelve Apostles*. These other documents allow us to look at the *Didache* as part of a developing liturgical tradition and to examine that tradition in terms of both source and redaction criticism. The two parts of the *Didache* itself give a reader the impression of two documents that have been edited into a single piece—a short catechetical document and a stylistically different liturgical document. In the mind of the editor or redactor, we might hypothesize, the catechesis of the "two ways" led religiously to the practices of the early church. This inference is supported by the Latin text from a later period, which translates only the document concerning the "two ways" and which leads toward the conclusion that the catechetical document did in fact exist in an independent form at some date prior to its diffusion from the Greek-speaking, eastern Mediterranean world to the Western, Latin-speaking lands. The later liturgical document, the *Constitutions*, can now also be recognized definitively as a product of redaction—granting the almost total inclusion of the *Didache* in it, augmented by other materials. By studying this redaction, we are able to assess the way in which liturgical and ministerial traditions develop over the course of time, by a process of modification and augmentation. The three related documents, taken together, present a picture of the developing life of the Christian church in its earliest centuries and, when interpreted in the context of other catechetical and liturgical documents from the same period, offer a picture of the variety of practices in the early church, together with some sense of their geographical specificity.

This hermeneutical circle of the critically armed interpreter, the text or document in question, and the context as learned from other sources contemporary with it, although fundamental to right interpretation, does not yet provide us with the whole picture or, more importantly, with a hermeneutical circle of which we as interpreters are genuinely, existentially, a part. On the one hand, this personal or existential dimension of interpretation ought to be viewed as somewhat perilous, while on the other, it must be recognized as absolutely necessary. Personal involvement with a text and its potential meaning may easily become a barrier to interpretation. We may be easily induced to import our own meanings, or meanings given to us by the community in which we belong, to a text or document. Nonetheless, without some existential involvement, the interpreter must ultimately be unable to perceive the significance of the text in its present-day location. In other words, there will be no reason for the interpretive exercise to take place, and no reason for the meaning of the text to be understood as relating either directly or indirectly to the present.

It is a simple fact of the world of writing and publishing that there are far more commentaries on the book of Isaiah than on the *Code of Hammurabi*, far more minds bent to the task of deciphering the prologue to the gospel of John than have worried through the discussion of the Demiurge in Plato's *Timaeus*. It is also obvious why this is the case. We take away nothing from the intrinsic worth of the *Code of Hammurabi* or of the *Timaeus* when we recognize that they play less of a role in the fashioning of the intellectual and spiritual identity of the contemporary Western or worldwide Christian community than do Isaiah and the gospel of John. Nor do we detract from the worth of Isaiah or the gospel of John if we note that the reverse was most certainly the case in ancient Mesopotamia and in the first and second centuries A.D.

It should be clear that neither the limited circle of the text and the exegete nor the somewhat expanded circle governed by the use of critical-historical tools and by a set of methodological criteria fully represents the work of the interpreter or provides the interpreter with the key to unlocking the present significance of the text. The work of the interpreter, whether biblical or church-historical, whether in a technically specialized field or in the larger, generalized, field of the communication of theology in ministry to the church, finally reaches out toward issues of present-day meaning, of the "application" or "significance" of a given text or document to the contemporary life-situation of the interpreter and his intended audience.

The term *significance* is probably preferable to the frequently heard "application" insofar as "application" bears the connotation of a somewhat artificial and necessarily adjunctive procedure accomplished in isolation from the basic work of interpretation, whereas "significance" connotes the discovery of a real relationship between the text and its context—including the new context provided by the work of the contemporary interpreter and the community of belief within which the text continues to have its normative function.

The necessary inclusion of the interpreter himself and of the community of belief in the hermeneutical circle once the issue of significance is raised points us toward a far larger circle—in fact, it points us toward the hermeneutical circle marked out by the fourfold curriculum of theology and its implication for the concrete task of doing theology in the contemporary church. The fourfold division of theology into biblical, historical, systematic, and practical theology identifies the larger hermeneutical circle within which Christian exegesis and theology operate and offers, in addition, a structure for understanding the norms of theology and their interrelationship. Once the critical task has been accomplished, a given text must be identified in terms of its place in the tradition as a whole—i.e., in its place as either a biblical, a church historical, or a contemporary systematic or practical statement. This whole, in turn, is the larger "whole" of which the text not only is a part, but is a part in relation to us in our present.

We not only identify the significance of texts differently, depending on whether they are biblical, church historical, or contemporary, we also understand texts differently, depending on the relationship between their context of understanding and our own. Modern hermeneutics recognized the role played in the work of interpretation by the self-understanding of the interpreter. The hermeneutical circle does not consist of a text or doctrine that stands in a particular context of meaning and an interpreter who exists without presuppositions, preunderstandings, or some inchoate relationship to the text chosen for interpretation.

The basic point has been made especially well by Anthony Thiselton in his discussion of the "two horizons" of interpretation.[13] Thiselton points out that older hermeneutics recognized the need of the interpreter to understand the historical and cultural context of the text or document but that it was only in the nineteenth century and, specifically, with Schleiermacher's approach to hermeneutics, that the historical and cultural context of the interpreter played a role in the understanding of a text. Or, as Thistleton states the issue:

> Understanding takes place when two sets of horizons are brought into relation to each other, namely those of the text and those of the interpreter. On this basis understanding presupposes a shared area of common perspectives, concepts or even judgments. . . . Since understanding new subject-matter still depends on a positive relation to the interpreter's own horizons, "lack of understanding is never totally removed." It constitutes a

---

[13]Anthony C. Thiselton, *The Two Horizons: New Testament Hermeneutics and Philosophical Description* (Grand Rapids: Eerdmans, 1980).

> progressive experience or process, not simply an act that can be definitively completed.[14]

In the interpretive process, the horizon of the text and the horizon of the interpreter interact, and the horizon of the interpreter is broadened as the meaning of the text comes to light and as it becomes significant in the present. The unreachable goal of the process is a "fusion of horizons"—unreachable because the context of the document being interpreted and the context of the interpreter can never become identical, no matter how clearly the former is understood by the latter.

In the contemporary formulation of theology, based as it must be on the findings of the past, the ongoing community of belief occupies a crucial place in the hermeneutical circle. It is precisely this historical community that provides a commonality of context and a concrete historical link between text and interpreter. In and through the historical community of belief, the horizon of the text maintains some existential relationship to the horizon of the interpreter, insofar as the text is interpreted anew from generation to generation and its ongoing significance in the tradition preserves elements of the original meaning. The historical record of faith and obedience, of theory and praxis, drawn out through the Old Testament, the New Testament, and the history of the church issues forth interpretively in contemporary theory and praxis—systematic and practical theology. The contemporary disciplines, in turn, look back interpretively into their biblical and historical roots, with the centuries of tradition intervening between the interpreter and a given text offering guidance concerning its meaning and its significance for the present.

The larger interpretive task, therefore, includes not only the initial work of exegesis that identifies the meaning of the text in its original context and the implications of that particular theological context for the somewhat larger structure of biblical theology. It also includes the movement through the theological and spiritual heritage of the community of belief into the present and, then, back again into the text. The theological

---

[14]Ibid., pp. 103–4, citing Schleiermacher, *Hermeneutik*, p. 141.

hermeneutic that goes on following the initial work of exegesis continually asks the question of how a particular point in biblical theology continues to lay claim, by means of the historical path of theory and praxis, to the church's present. The historical creeds and confessions of the church not only offer crucial indications of the way in which the text lays claim on the life and thought of the community, they also provide pathways back into the text from the present. By asking, in a final contemporizing step of interpretation, how the text has led the community of belief to particular credal and confessional conclusions, we open the text on a different level to our own theological concerns.

At a previous point in this study, we noted that the Johannine prologue does not easily yield up language of essence, person, and intra-Trinitarian relationships. Indeed, it would be a terrible mistake for exegesis to assume the Nicene language as a presupposition to interpretation. Nonetheless, once the exegesis has been done and we have understood as best we can the first-century implications of logos-language, we must ask the further question of why this text rather than other New Testament texts is drawn to our attention as a focus for theological formulation. Not the least among the reasons for this attention is that logos-language was crucial to the contextualization of the gospel in the second century, when the apologists recognized the significance of logos to the surrounding culture and made the Johannine prologue central to the church's work of communicating the gospel.

Once we have recognized this issue, we then can move forward toward an understanding of the church's endeavor to hold fast to its monotheistic faith while at the same time doing justice to the ideal of an immanent divine Logos sent forth into the world. The church not only fastened on to the Johannine term *monogenēs*, "unique," or as traditionally rendered, "only-begotten," but also used this term in order to maintain the full divinity of the Logos. The adaptation idea of "begetting" to the discussion of the inner workings of the Godhead, helpful in identifying a distinction between God as such and the Logos sent forth into the world, also caused a certain difficulty for monotheism. The church needed to make clear that this begetting did not mirror human begetting and did not result in the generation of a quasi-divine being separate from God. Following the third century, the idea of an "eternal begetting"—of an internal, eternal, distinction of logos from the divine essence as such—arose as a way of resolving the dilemma of the language.

In our own theological efforts this element of traditional churchly Trinitarianism, although not a direct exegetical result of the text, becomes an important element in the subsequent interpretive work of understanding the text in our present context—particularly granting the continuing importance of the fundamental confession of the presence of God in Christ reconciling the world to himself. The church's Trinitarian creeds and confessions enter the hermeneutical circle, following exegesis, as an essential element in the appropriation of the text in and for our confessing present. This remains the case inasmuch as the basic exegesis of the text, prior to the investigation of the creeds and confessions, will raise questions about the relation of logos-language and of incarnation to our monotheism not at all unlike the questions already encountered by the early church. The church's previous meditation on these issues—in view of its doctrinal intentions, even more than because of its specific terminological results—is crucial to our understanding of the function of the text in our own faith today.

CONTEXTUALIZATION AND THE INTERPRETIVE TASK

The term *contextualization* is a relatively new addition to the theological vocabulary. It points toward a new sensitivity to the problem of bringing the message of Christianity to bear on faith and life in the present. The message of the gospel arose in one cultural, social, historical, and linguistic context, and we live in another. Those to whom the church attempts to bring the message of the gospel live in yet another cultural, social, historical, and linguistic context: for, even as our histories converge in this "global village" and become intertwined, the variety of the past continues to affect our future, as do the divergent cultures and languages of the world.

In order for the gospel to become meaningful to us in our own present life-situation and to others in different places and different cultures in their distinctive life-situations, it must be brought into the diverse contexts of the modern world. It must be contextualized. It ought to be made clear that the work of contextualization has been a part of the interpretive task of the church throughout the ages: contextualization occurred—with incredible success—when the essentially Palestinian phenomenon of earliest Christianity moved out into the gentile mission and became the faith first of the Greek-speaking world of the ancient Mediterranean basin and then of the Latin world of the western Mediterranean. It occurred again as Christianity was brought to the barbarian kingdoms beyond the bounds of the Roman Empire, and to the barbarian rulers who became the lords of Rome—and it has occurred again with enormous diversity of expression in the spread of Christianity to sub-Saharan Africa and to Asia. In other words, contextualization is one of the basic elements of the life, spread, and survival of Christianity.

The newness of the term *contextualization*, however, points us to the fact that this age-old interpretive exercise has been recognized, analyzed, and *consciously* attempted only recently. There are at least three basic reasons for this fact. First, the process of contextualization has gone on so long and so successfully in the West, at least until recently, that it has tended to become culturally invisible. Christianity, as interpreted by the early, medieval, and Reformation church, is so imbedded in our culture that the cultural differences between the ancient culture presented in Scripture and the civilization of the West are at times difficult to discern. And those differences that do appear are easily explained as belonging to the development of culture from its ancient origins toward the modern, scientific world. Contextualization, as a cultural problem, becomes readily visible only when the gospel is interpreted in different terms by divergent cultures that are also in dialogue with one another.

Second, the modern missionary efforts of Western churches, from their sixteenth-century beginnings onward, were just as imperialistic as the expansion and colonization efforts that brought the missions. The underlying assumption of mission work during most of its history has been that Western Christianity needed to be superimposed on other cultures and the Christianity of native populations conformed to Western standards. Any deviation from the Western model—even if undertaken in the name of the gospel—was viewed as a declension from the truth. Granting the historical difficulty of recognizing one's own faith as a contextualization and recognizing the historical presence, noted previously, of Christianity at the heart of the development of Western culture, this imperialistic approach, if not ultimately justifiable, is surely understandable. Christianization was confused with westernization. Only recently have we become sensitive to the possibility of different formulations of the gospel grounded in different cultural contexts.

This new cultural awareness leads us to the third point: the development of Western hermeneutics has led, in the last century and a half, to an understanding of patterns of interpretation that recognizes the fact of contextualization and the relationship of contextualization to a larger frame of reference. The significance of a document or concept in a new context arises out of the relationship already existing between the interpreter's self-understanding and the framework of understanding lodged in the document or concept. By way of example, a text from the Bible attains significance in the present far more surely and certainly than an ancient Babylonian religious text because the Western, Christian interpreter, before any work of interpretation, stands in a cultural and historical relationship to the biblical text. We are able to contextualize or re-contextualize the biblical message because, at a fundamental level, that message has had a long-term impact on our culture.

In accordance not only with this view of contextualization but also with the approach to theology that we have been developing throughout this study, contemporary Christians must find a way to affirm their theologies—including their theological systems—that does justice both to the absoluteness of the divine object of theology and the relativity of its contemporary forms. Christians tend, all too much like the missionaries of preceding centuries, to view their own confessional or theological system as an absolute, that is, as the only possible form that can be taken by the biblical message. The point is not that there is a problem with the systematic presentation of theology and not that, within a given culture or society, this presentation ought to strive for diversity of expression (as if diversity in and of itself were a virtue). Nor is it the point that, within a particular culture, no single systematic presentation may be arguably better than another. Systematic presentation itself is valuable, perhaps even necessary; and it is clearly possible that, within a given culture or society, one systematic presentation will best express the biblical message at the heart of Christianity.

A problem arises when a particular system or a particular grouping of systematic presentations is so identified with the biblical message that the transmission of the message either to another culture or society or to another phase or era of the same culture or society becomes extremely difficult if not impossible. In other words, one way of stating the message can become absolutized, usually because it has been a highly effective and successful formulation, with the result that a culturally conditioned theological statement is transmitted to and forced upon a cultural situation in which it cannot function. The historical course of Western Christianity in its chronological length, intellectual breadth, and conceptual depth offers us a multitude of examples of the problem and of its solution. Rather than view the history of Western Christianity as the gradual and progressive construction of the ultimate theological system, we ought to view it as a laboratory of successful contextualization, indeed, of a series of such contextualizations.

Thus understood, the work of contextualization is little more than the self-conscious exercise of a form of historical method for the sake of the present-day statement of the faith.

The result of an effective contextualization of the Christian message is no more and no less than the adaptation of the substance of Christian teaching to a new linguistic and cultural life situation. The result of a successful exercise in historical criticism is no more and no less than the understanding of the meaning of Christian teaching in a past linguistic and cultural life situation. It should be clear that the present-day effort to contextualize a historical faith rests on an ability to grasp the meaning of the faith in its basic forms by means of historical method. Contextualization, therefore, when it becomes a conscious exercise, is part of a historically controlled exercise in hermeneutics.

Atonement theory provides an excellent series of examples for discussion. The New Testament provides not one but several ways of describing the atoning work of Christ: it is a ransom paid for sin, a sacrificial expiation of sin, a substitutionary act that puts Christ in our place under the divine punishment for sin; it is the victory of Christ over the powers of evil; it is the redemptive manifestation of divine love; it is the act of the second man or new Adam becoming the head of redeemed humanity in Adam's place. All of these approaches to atonement can be found in the New Testament and all, most probably, can be linked exegetically to the demand of particular life-situations on the preaching and interpretation of the gospel. They are, thus, not to be viewed as mutually exclusive, nor are they to be viewed as easily harmonizable into a single theory. Throughout the history of the church, theologians and churchmen have drawn selectively on these models of atonement and have brought the gospel to bear on various situations and contexts in which, perhaps, not all of the various models would have been readily understood.

In a culture that well recognized the corporate character of human identity and responsibility and the representative character of monarchs and heads of households—and that universally accepted a more or less allegorical and typological reading of sacred texts—Irenaeus of Lyons looked at the various ways in which the New Testament had defined Christ's work and selected, not the language of sacrifice or ransom, but rather the language of "first" and "second man," the "old" and the "new Adam," as the foundation of his preaching of salvation. His so-called Recapitulation Theory is literally a theory of new headship (*anakephaliosis*; re-capitu-lation) or repetition in one individual, of the corporate development of the race.

Against the Gnostics, Irenaeus could argue that the human predicament is not the result of a cosmic dualism, of a good and an evil ultimate engaged in battle, of the entrapment of elements of the good—souls—in the evil realm of matter, but rather the result of an all-too-human catastrophe, the sinful disobedience of the first head of the human race. Redemption is made possible by the creation of a new corporate humanity gathered under a new head—the second man, the new Adam, Jesus Christ. In order to argue this model for Christ's atoning and reconciling work, Irenaeus looked at the stories of Adam's defeat and Christ's victory and, allegorically and typologically, demonstrated that the story of Christ undoes, in a recapitulatory mirror-image repetition, the story of Adam. Adam brought the race into sin at the instance of the virgin Eve; Christ brought the race into salvation through the instrumentality of the virgin Mary. Adam sinned in taking fruit from a tree; Christ brought redemption nailed to a tree. As we all fell in Adam, so do we all rise in Christ. The basic paradigm is Pauline—the elaboration is Irenaean and capable of speaking to the social and corporate understanding of the late second century.

Other writers of Irenaeus' day and throughout the patristic era selected other New Testament themes, such as our bondage to "the god of this age" (2 Cor. 4:4) or the similar theme of Christ's victory over the powers (cf. Rom. 8:37–39; Col. 2:8, 14–15)—again, not because these themes necessarily appeared to them to be the central themes of the New Testament in its own right, but because this particular New Testament way of understanding Christ's work spoke directly to their own cultural and historical context. In the Christian apologetic tradition, from the mid–second century onward, the early church had to confront a polytheistic world with a monotheistic message of salvation. In doing so, the fathers did not deny the existence of the pagan gods; instead, much like the

Old Testament, they demoted the gods of the pagan nations and interpreted them as lesser beings—indeed, as demons, principalities and powers of the spiritual world. The New Testament message of Christ's victory over the powers, over the "god of this age," was easily adapted to the cultural situation as a message of the divine agency in Christ offering victory over the many and often capricious deities of the pagan world.

As well as these two models of atonement theory served the early church, they did not seem adequate to communicate the gospel to the altered social and cultural situation of the Middle Ages. The problem of polytheism still existed on the edges of Christianity, but, in contrast to the culture of the ancient world, the culture of the Middle Ages was officially Christian and monotheistic. In a general sense at least, granting that polytheism was no longer a recognized cultural option by the end of the eleventh century, that evil spiritual powers could be dealt with by other means than atonement theory, and that the corporate understanding of the social order and of the place of human beings in it had changed considerably, the language of Christ's work was in need of a new model, a model capable of communicating the gospel in a different context.

The great treatise of Anselm of Canterbury on the logic of incarnation and atonement, the *Cur Deus Homo* (*Why the God-Man?*), argued the inadequacy of the patristic theories of atonement and pressed the question not simply of the meaning of atonement but of the way in which Christ's identity as Mediator points toward the underlying logic of salvation. Anselm attacked the notion that Christ's death was a payment made to Satan, the god of this world: why, after all, should payment be made to one to whom nothing is rightly owed? Satan does indeed exercise power over human beings, but that power is wrongly gained and unjustly exercised. No payment, therefore, is necessary to break his power. Nonetheless, Christ's work does have the character of a transaction, and the human disobedience for which Christ atones does stand as a debt that must be paid. The debt is a debt of obedience—indeed, argues Anselm, it is the obedience originally and perpetually owed by human beings to God. Our plight is that we, locked in our sinfulness and disobedience, are unable to pay God what we owe.

Apart from Christ we stand before God as debtors. We owe an obedience that we cannot pay. Nor can God simply overlook the problem: by failing to pay obedient homage to God we have in fact dishonored God's name. The debt must be paid and God's honor restored before the human race can enjoy renewed fellowship with God. It was clear to Anselm that only a human being could repay the debt: it would hardly be fitting for a human debt to be paid by an angelic being! It was equally clear that no sinful human being is capable of making such a payment both because no individual debtor, himself in jeopardy, is capable of paying the debt of others, and because the enormity of sin is such that no human being is capable of satisfying the debt. Satisfaction must, therefore, be made by a member of the human race who is somehow free from its sinfulness and who somehow transcends its limitations. Such a person is the God-man, Jesus Christ—born sinless of the virgin Mary and incarnate God in union with human nature. The divine-human person of Christ is, thus, suitable to the task of atonement or, as Anselm would say, satisfaction.

Such, in a nutshell, was Anselm's theory. We recognize in it many of the elements of the standard orthodox Protestant penal substitution theory, but we note also substantial differences in language. Rather than a language of vicarious substitution for punishment, Anselm offers a language of satisfaction made to the divine honor. Theologians have often observed, usually in order to discredit Anselm's theory, that the logic of his argument is not so much biblical as medieval and that the picture of sinners having failed to pay a debt of honor is very much like the picture of a medieval vassal who has fallen short of the obligation he owes to his feudal lord. The satisfaction exacted either from the disobedient vassal (eternal punishment in the case of God's human "vassals") or from a substitute, a champion, is a legal model drawn from medieval feudal practice. Anselm's theological critics, together with the critics of the Anselmian elements that remain in the penal substitution theory, typically argue against its excessive legalism and its "medieval" character.

Far from being a problem for atonement theory or for theology in general, however, Anselm's use of feudal legal imagery is a perfect example of successful contextualization. The atoning work of Christ, which none of the gospel writers and none of the fathers of the church could have conceived of in precisely this manner, has been beautifully presented in the language and the logic of the late eleventh century. Earlier centuries—and later ones—may have little contact with Anselm's language of honor and satisfaction, with its hints of lords and vassals, but Anselm's century and the centuries immediately following found in this terminology the basis of a suitable way of making the work of Christ intelligible, a point of departure for an adequate contextualization of the message, capable of establishing in a language suitable to its time, the objective achievement of Christ on the cross.

Modern-day critics of Anselm's feudal metaphors have not undermined Anselm's achievement at all. What they have done is to recognize that it no longer represents Christ's atonement to us in terms that partake of the very fabric of our lives and our cultural context, and that a new and altered language of atonement is needed. Critics of the Anselmian view also seem to forget that it did not enter the stream of developing Christian doctrine without challenge and modification and that both the challenge (from Abelard) and the modification (at the hands of Lombard, Aquinas, and others) tell us something about the way in which Christian doctrine can be successfully contextualized. It must be debated through the eyes of individuals and groups immersed in the culture of the time.

Anselm's atonement theory also points us toward a crucial issue in our understanding of theological language. Theological language is not a special, exalted language delivered by God and preserved somehow from involvement in the world. Theological language is ordinary language, and it follows the rules of ordinary language. Theology can be intelligible only when it speaks the linguistic coin of the realm. Using Augustine's or Anselm's or Calvin's or Wesley's language in an era unaccustomed to their usage is like trying to buy lunch in Chicago with a handful of German marks. The coinage is valuable, but not useful in Chicago. What Anselm did for atonement theory was to express it in the linguistic currency of the eleventh and early twelfth centuries. As in all theological usage, he took terms and concepts that had, previously, only a secular and a legal meaning, and he shifted their focus, enlarging their range of meaning to include a religious dimension.

Any time that theology crosses a cultural boundary, whether historical or geographical, new terms and new metaphors must be drawn out of the spiritual, intellectual, and linguistic storehouse of the culture and adapted for use in Christian theology. There is, of course, no ready-made formula, no standard blueprint, for making this crosscultural transition and bringing about a successful contextualization of the message. History has demonstrated, especially in the history of the early church, that the enormously difficult passage from one linguistically identified cultural form to another is fraught with problems—indeed, with heresies—and is successfully traversed primarily by bilingual thinkers whose life-experience has given them a close acquaintance with both cultures. We see such transmitters and translators in the apostle Paul, Tertullian, and Hilary of Poitiers, each of whom, particularly Paul and Tertullian, was responsible for a language of theology fundamental to our Western form of Christianity, so fundamental that we can hardly conceive of Christianity apart from their vocabulary. From Paul we have, among other things, our language of grace, faith, and justification; from Tertullian we receive the Trinitarian/Christological terminology of person and nature.

The contextualization of theology is both an objective and a subjective, both a corporate and an individual exercise. On one level, it is an exercise performed by Christians every day. When a Christian family prays at mealtime, particularly if the prayer is not one of the standard blessings typically repeated on such occasions but is an extemporaneous prayer that reflects the present moment and its concerns, the contextualization of the Christian message has occurred. The same can be said of an effective sermon, a visitation of the sick, a counseling session, and a rudimentary application of the Christian moral principles in everyday life. In each of these exercises, two basic functions of theological thinking and living have taken place. On the one hand, some basic truth or principle held by the larger, historical and contemporary community of faith has been interpreted in relation to a new and highly particularized context or life-situation. On the other hand, the interpretive work is paralleled by and, in fact, completed in an inward appropriation of the message—the truth, the principle—through which the believer is enabled to understand her context religiously. Daily religious activities, in other words, are predicated on a hermeneutical and spiritual exercise.

Everything that we said about the study of language, about the interpretive and self-interpretive encounter via language with different worlds of thought, and about the necessity of grappling with the extracanonical or larger cultural context of a theology applies directly to the work of contextualization in the present. Contextualization is nothing other than the "pre-sentizing" conclusion of the hermeneutical task, the completion of the hermeneutical circle in our own persons and in the context of present-day existence. The more successful the exercise in addressing both the meaning of the original text or doctrine and drawing it forward toward a contemporary significance that respects the intention of the original formulator but also serves the religious needs of the present, the more the hermeneutical circle has led to a broadening of the interpreter's religious and spiritual horizon in and through the "fusion" of her horizon with that of the text or doctrine.

From the point of view of the hermeneutical procedure, then, contextualization means the widening of the present horizon, the addition of yet another interpretive context or life-situation to the historical pattern of interpretation. In other words, contextualization is also the "cutting edge" of the tradition of the believing community as it moves into and engages with the present situation. The original biblical or churchly meaning does not change, but the text, the document, the doctrine, the idea or principle in question attains a significance in a new context and, therefore, to a certain extent, attains a new significance related to the old and, at the same time, broadens the horizon of the believing community in the present.

The limitations of interpretation that we recognized earlier now come into play. The hermeneutical circle of interpreter and text created anew by a new address to a doctrinal issue in a new context of belief must be legitimized—it must be a churchly circle linking the interpreter to the text in and through the historical path that has linked the text to the interpreter. It must be a circle that establishes the boundaries of significance without preventing the reception of the text into the life of the present community. The "new" significance, therefore, cannot ever be entirely new: rather it is a dimension of interpretation, arising from a particular context, that draws on the original meaning of the text but also on its tradition of meaning and that, without negating the past, draws that rich realm of interpretation into a new present.

The point is simply that the present significance of the text or doctrine must not only be rooted in its original meaning, but that its rootage can be guaranteed in only one place—in the ongoing life of the historical community in which the text or doctrine first came into being. A text or doctrine that does *not* belong to the ongoing life of the historical community of belief of which the interpreter is a part cannot easily be drawn significantly into the present situation. By way of example, the following passage from "The Surangama Sutra" makes very little religious sense to the Western Christian mind and spirit and, even with lengthy interpretation, has little chance of attaining the significance of Psalm 23 or the prologue to the gospel of John:

> Ananda replied:—You are now asking me about the existence of my mind. To answer that question I must use my thinking and reasoning faculty to search and find an answer. Yes, now I understand. This thinking and reasoning being is what is meant as "my mind."

The Lord Buddha rebuked Ananda sharply and said:—surely that is nonsense, to assert that your being is your mind. . . . [This] is simply one of the false conceptions that arises from reflecting about the relations of yourself and outside objects, which obscures your true and essential Mind. It is because, since from beginningless time down to the present life, you have been constantly misunderstanding your true and essential Mind. It is like treating a petty thief as your own son. By so doing you have lost consciousness of your original and permanent mind and because of it have been forced to undergo the sufferings of successive deaths and rebirths.[15]

The editor of the volume from which this quotation is taken, Lin Yutang, characterizes "The Surangama Sutra" as "a kind of *Essay on Human Understanding* and *Gospel of St. John* combined, with the intellectual force of the one and the religious spirit of the other."[16]

The Western Christian interpreter—without passing any judgment whatsoever on the religious and philosophical teachings present in the above text—would not have much success in attempting to draw out of "The Surangama Sutra" a significance for himself for his community of belief. Granting that the horizon of the interpreter is determined by the somewhat broader horizon of the community in which he lives and believes, and that the horizon of the community is determined by its own historical and cultural trajectory, this text from another community with its own utterly distinct historical and cultural trajectory simply does not speak in the new, Western context, certainly not with the power and significance with which it speaks in its own Eastern context.

From a hermeneutical and contextual perspective, therefore, there is no question that the "presuppositional" approach to theology carries the day against a purely "evidential" approach. As we noted briefly in the discussion of apologetics in the previous chapter, there is always a sense in which explana-

---

[15]From "The Surangama Sutra," in *The Wisdom of China and India*, edited by Lin Yutang (New York: Random House, 1942), p. 512.

[16]Ibid., p. 491.

tion and defense of a theological point must follow the doctrinal declaration of the point. This is not to say that our beliefs need not be rational or that they ought not to be supported by sound evidences, but only that the rational proofs and the historical or empirical evidences are seldom if ever the reason for belief. They are, however, to paraphrase Anselm, the foundation of subsequent understanding. We come to a text or a doctrine with predispositions, rooted in our community of belief and formed by a particular cultural context and historical situation.

The presence of the tradition also makes possible a pattern of mutual enlightenment between different cultural and historical expressions of the Christian message. Interpretation of the gospel in a Latin American or Asian or African context, insofar as it remains true to the basic intention of the church in its preaching and insofar as it has arisen out of the tradition that bears the text and brings it into each new situation, can be significant not only to the life of the culture into which the gospel has been newly brought but also to the tradition as a whole. Just as present-day exegesis and application draw on an understanding of two historical and cultural moments—that of the text and that of the modern-day interpreter—so also can the encounter of two acculturated or contextualized interpretations shed light on both and on the meaning of the text as well.

EPILOGUE: THE STUDY OF THEOLOGY AS AN EXERCISE IN CHRISTIAN CULTURE

Much of what has already been said in this and the preceding chapters has tended not only toward the thesis that hermeneutics and spirituality are closely linked but also toward its corollary, the realization that spirituality is a characteristic of the entire study of theology and not simply a subject that can be studied or an exercise in "Christian personal formation" that can be tacked on to a curriculum or on to the individual, personal study of theology. One of the great virtues of Farley's *Theologia* is that it draws attention to the older model of theology as consisting in part of a "disposition" or *habitus* for theological knowing.[17] In this model, as both the medieval and the post-Reformation Protestant treatments of the method or *ratio* for the study of theology invariably indicate, theology involved not only the examination of ideas and documents but also the cultivation of the spiritual, attitudinal life of the individual. Johann Heinrich Alsted, writing in the early seventeenth century, even argued the necessary relation between a healthy mind and a healthy body and prescribed good physical care for students of theology—a point, we note, that has been profoundly neglected in modern theological study.

The assumption of the older study of theology was that the exegetical study of Scripture in the original languages, the meditation on classic works of theology by thinkers like Athanasius, Augustine, Anselm, Aquinas, Luther, and Calvin, and the careful contemplation of the technical language of dogmatics could and ought to be a spiritually uplifting experience— inasmuch as the student would be trained by such study in a regimen of meditation on the "things of God," that is, on God and God's works of creation and redemption. It was also assumed, not only in the study of theology, but in education in general, certainly through the nineteenth century, that the exercise of the mind in worthy subjects brought with it the upbuilding of character. History and philosophy were to be studied, not only because they were important for the intellectual background of the "educated person" but also because they inculcated wisdom concerning human nature, its heights and its depths. Equally so, and, indeed, even more, ought the study of the "things of God"—of the history and thought of the community of belief—be experienced as the inculcation of a spiritually enlightening wisdom, of a way of life as well as a pattern of thought.

This sense of the confluence of theological formulation and personal formation in the rightly ordered study of theology is hardly an academic pipedream. It is a foundational principle of spirituality recognized in our times by a writer as well known

---

[17]Cf. Edward Farley, *Theologia: The Fragmentation and Unity of Theological Education* (Philadelphia: Fortress, 1983), pp. 31–39.

in the realm of piety and spirituality as A. W. Tozer. Tozer began one of his best-loved works with the lament that "the Church has surrendered her once lofty concept of God" and that with this "loss of the sense of majesty has come the further loss of religious awe and consciousness of the divine Presence."[18] Tozer notes with irony the "dramatic gains" in wealth and size of churches—external gains that are paralleled by "internal losses" in the "quality of our religion." He offers his book as pointing toward a solution to the problem and then adds, "Were Christians today reading such works as those of Augustine and Anselm a book like this would have no reason for being."[19]

When Tozer looked to the wellsprings of his own spirituality and to the basis of a solution to the church's spiritual dilemma, he looked to the giants of the history of theology, to thinkers who gave not only to the church but also to Western culture both substance and inspiration. In Augustine and Anselm, Tozer found two writers in whom theology and spirituality were one and the same, who identified theological study both as the search for truth and as the identification of the good and the approach to God. In the thought of these and other theologians of the past, God, Being, the good, and truth were assumed to be identical—so that the study of theology was also an examination of foundational principles of the natural order, of ethics, and of philosophy.

In other words, the study of theology, in the classical sense, is a study of values or, more precisely, of a fairly well-defined body of materials that, in their primary intention, communicate values—values to be believed and values to be acted upon. If, on the one hand, the historical method of examining and analyzing the biblical and church historical materials serves to locate their grammatical meaning and original cultural significance within a particular historical, cultural, social, and religious context (and, to a certain extent,

---

[18]A. W. Tozer, *The Knowledge of the Holy: The Attributes of God: Their Meaning in Christian Life* (San Francisco: Harper & Row, 1961), p. vii.

[19]Ibid., pp. vii–viii.

relativize the documents), our membership, on the other hand, in the ongoing community of belief that locates its identity in the tradition of these materials places us in a position to receive the truths and the values expressed in the materials as our own. The historical relativity of the form of expression does not in any way detract from the ultimacy of the values toward which the particular form of expression points.

Study of the materials of the church—the various historical forms in which the community has expressed its beliefs and formulated its ethical standards—becomes an exercise in the expression of one's own beliefs and the formulation of one's own standards. The cultural and social relativity of the documents serves, moreover, in the exercise, to press us toward our own statement of these corporately held values, insofar as we recognize both the limitation of the particular cultural form and the ultimacy of the values expressed under it.

Although no one should dispute that any of the theological disciplines—whether biblical, historical, systematic, or practical—represents an intellectual and a spiritual effort, conducted with attention to a theoretical as well as to a practical dimension, for the sake of developing a clearer understanding of the nature and the subject of the discipline, it is historical theology and systematic theology that suffer the greatest pressures in our time from the anti–intellectualist spirit. How often do we hear, in many different forms and phrases, the complaint that such "theoretical" disciplines are divorced from the spiritual life of Christianity and place barriers in the way of piety? How often do we hear that emphasis on abstract formulae is a "Greek" way of thinking that ought not to be imposed on the "Hebraic" faith of the gospel? How often have we heard that mind, the intellect, the "head," ought not to displace the "heart"—as if the heart (with profuse apologies to William Harvey!) were actually the seat of the emotions? We hear these complaints so frequently and some of their presuppositions are so ingrained into the contemporary religious psyche, that the simple mention of them has the force of argument in some quarters—and any argument against them will be faced with considerable opposition from the outset. Yet the argument must be mounted if the faith is to survive and if our theology and spirituality are to be understood and appreciated for what they actually are.

The discussion of hermeneutics and contextualization points toward what may well be the basic question that needs to be addressed in the study of theology as it moves from the historically defined biblical foundations of Christianity toward contemporary formulation: Does the theological result of any individual effort at formulation both address and inform the culture within which that formulation has taken place? Granting the long history of the Judeo-Christian tradition, any statement of the contemporary significance of our basic beliefs and values will be an experiment in the crosscultural transmission of theology and in the contextualization or, indeed, recontextualization of particular teachings of the believing community. The success of Christianity and its great gift to the world cannot simply be defined in the standard theological language of the salvation of the individual; they must also be defined in terms of the formation of Western culture.

Our culture is, of course, not entirely Christian or Judeo-Christian. It is also profoundly Greek and Roman, Anglo-Saxon and Germanic—and in the twentieth century increasingly influenced by the thoughts, tastes, and sounds of the Far East. But Christianity has not merely been one component of this larger cultural experience. It has also been the preserver, mediator, and interpreter of the other ancient elements of Western culture. We do not, in other words, experience a cultural tradition internally at odds with itself, consisting in many unrelated streams or trajectories, but instead a cultural tradition that has tended to draw the wealth of past ages together into the service of its present. Much of this work has been the work of Christianity.

What the Christianity of the past has done, time and time again, has been to give to Western culture a sense of historical and moral direction, a structure of values, an identification of the ultimate good, and a coherent view of reality. There have, of course, been moments of grave difficulty. The rediscovery of the physical and metaphysical works of Aristotle in the early thirteenth century created a problem of the first order: here was what seemed to be an alternative worldview. Similarly, the discoveries of Copernicus, Kepler, and Galileo appeared to fracture the Christian worldview. But in both cases, theology was able to adapt: the so-called Thomistic synthesis of Aristotelian philosophy and Christian theology remains a monument to formulation in both fields of inquiry. And as for the heliocentric solar system, it was integrated quite easily into a fairly traditional view of the relationship of God and world, finally proving to be not at all the monster it once seemed to be.

In both cases, and in numerous others, we can see both the resilience of the core of Christian theology and piety and the ability of the church's fundamental teachings to address a changing society. Whatever our differences or disagreements with the exegetical methods and doctrinal formulations of past ages, it remains true that the church in other times was capable both of recognizing the needs and addressing the issues of the contemporary cultural situation—and capable, also, of recognizing the fundamental intention of its doctrinal formulations as, sometimes, distinct from the language in which they had been stated. Exegetes and theologians of the past, as illustrated in this volume, were able, by means of the methods of interpretation available to them in their time, to draw together the whole of theology—the biblical and historical materials, contemporary statement and practice—into forms capable of addressing the needs of individuals, of the community of belief, and of the larger culture around it.

The great difficulty of theological formulation today, and the great difficulty of the relevance of theological formulation to the present life of Western culture stems in no small part from a failure of intellectual and spiritual nerve in the church in the twentieth century. The clergyman of my introductory chapter, however expert a technician or operations manager he may be, is not a bearer of culture. He may be able to organize a group in the present and he may be able to offer many of its members all of the emotional solace they need, but he will leave their children spiritually impoverished. The theology that he set aside in the name of practice is nothing more or less than the cultural heritage of the church, the tools for a Christian construction not just of a congregational body but of a view of God and world, of ultimate reality, of our universe and the place of human beings in it.

The task of theological formulation in the present day is to draw together into an interpretive unity the various elements of theology and to produce, from within the community of faith, a contemporary science of the Christian religion that recognizes as its proper object the construction of a view of reality suitable to the perpetuation of Christian culture. This is a very tall order. It calls not only for a general mastery, on the part of clergy and teachers, of the various elements of the "diversified encyclopedia," it also calls for an attentiveness to the way in which these elements fit together, for a responsibility both to the larger faith of the ongoing Christian community and to the needs of objective or "scientific" study. In addition, it calls for a willingness to use the materials of doctrine, the biblical and historical sources, not as gatherings of right statements that need only to be repeated but as foundations for contemporary formulation in contemporary language and in response to a contemporary situation.

FOR FURTHER READING

A complete list of works cited may be found in the index of authors and titles. In the following bibliographical discussion I have noted works that will be particularly significant and helpful in the task of understanding the pattern and organization of theological study.

The theological disciplines are analyzed and surveyed in such classic works on "encyclopedia" as: J. F. Räbiger, *Encyclopaedia of Theology*, 2 vols., trans. J. Macpherson (Edinburgh: T & T Clark, 1884–1885), a work valuable for its critical analysis of other "encyclopedias" of its day; Philip Schaff, *Theological Propaedeutic: A General Introduction to the Study of Theology, Exegetical, Historical, Systematic, and Practical* (New York: Scribner, 1894), a classic study, still valuable for its survey of the fields and their relationships (as with many of the nineteenth-century efforts, its greatest weakness is on the "practical" side); George R. Crooks and John F. Hurst, *Theological Encyclopaedia and Methodology, on the basis of Hagenbach*, new ed., rev. (New York: Hunt and Eaton, 1894), perhaps the best of the nineteenth-century encyclopedias; Alfred Cave, *An Introduction to Theology: Its Principles, Its Branches, Its Results and Its Literature* (Edinburgh: T. & T. Clark, 1886); Gerald Birney Smith, ed., *A Guide to the Study of the Christian Religion* (Chicago: University of Chicago Press, 1916), a classic "liberal" introduction to the theological encyclopedia from the point of view of the study of religion, written by some of the outstanding scholars of its time; Kenneth E. Kirk, *The Study of Theology* (London: Hodder and Stoughton, 1939), and Daniel T. Jenkins, ed., *The Scope of Theology* (Cleveland and New York: World, 1965), multi-authored works that offer sound essays on most of the fields of theology; and Gerhard Ebeling, *The Study of Theology*, trans. Duane Priebe (Philadelphia: Fortress, 1978), the best modern survey of the various fields.

The seminal contemporary studies of theology, its various disciplines and the problem of the unity of theological study are Edward Farley, *Theologia: The Fragmentation and Unity of Theological Education* (Philadelphia: Fortress, 1983) and Wolfhart Pannenberg, *Theology and the Philosophy of Science*, trans. Francis McDonagh (Philadelphia: Westminster, 1976), both discussed at length in the appendix to chapter 1, above. A useful introduction to Pannenberg's theology is his *Basic Questions in Theology:*

Collected Essays, trans. George H. Kehm, 2 vols. (Philadelphia: Fortress, 1970–1971; repr. Philadelphia: Westminster, 1983).

The histories of the various theological disciplines and of the ideas of theology and its encyclopedia are discussed, in addition to the presentations in Crooks and Hurst, *Encyclopedia*, and Schaff, *Theological Propaedeutic*, in Charles Augustus Briggs, *History of the Study of Theology*, 2 vols. (London: Duckworth, 1916); Yves M.-J. Congar, *A History of Theology*, trans. Hunter Guthrie (Garden City: Doubleday, 1968), a valuable survey of the history of the idea of theology, especially useful as a survey of the meaning and implications of "theology" in the patristic and medieval periods; John H. Hayes and Frederick Prussner, *Old Testament Theology: Its History and Development* (Atlanta: John Knox, 1985), and Werner Georg Kümmel, *The New Testament: The History of the Investigation of Its Problems*, trans. S. McLean Gilmour and Howard C. Kee (Nashville and New York: Abingdon, 1972), highly useful studies of the character and development of biblical theology; Louis Berkhof, *Introduction to Systematic Theology* (Grand Rapids: Eerdmans, 1932; repr. Baker, 1979), and Revere Franklin Weidner, *Introduction to Dogmatic Theology. Based on Luthardt,* (Rock Island, Ill.: Augustana Book Concern, 1888), surveys of the history and method of theology, serving as prolegomena to dogmatics. Noteworthy among the histories of the practical disciplines are Edwin Charles Dargan, *A History of Preaching*, vol. 1, *From the Apostolic Fathers to the Great Reformers, A.D. 70–1572*; vol. 2, *From the Close of the Reformation to the End of the Nineteenth Century, 1572–1900*, 2 vols. in one (repr. Grand Rapids: Baker, 1954); Bernard Cooke, *Ministry to Word and Sacraments: History and Theology* (Philadelphia: Fortress, 1976); William A. Clebsch and Charles B. Jaekle, *Pastoral Care in Historical Perspective* (New York: Harper & Row, 1967); and John T. McNeill, *A History of the Cure of Souls* (New York: Harper and Brothers, 1951).

In addition to the above noted studies, various issues and aspects of theological method are discussed in Abraham Kuyper, *Principles of Sacred Theology*, trans. De Vries, with an intro. by Benjamin B. Warfield (Grand Rapids: Baker, 1980), a classic Reformed study of the meaning of theology and the method of dogmatics; Paul Avis, *The Methods of Modern Theology* (Basingstoke: Marshall Pickering, 1986) a work containing useful discussions of Schleiermacher, Barth, Tillich, and other "makers of modern theology"; Carl E. Braaten, *History and Hermeneutics* (Philadelphia: Westminster, 1966); Van A. Harvey, *The Historian and the Believer* (New York: Macmillan, 1969), a good introduction to the problems of historical method used in the context of exegesis and belief; Edwin A. Burtt, "The Problem of Theological Method," in *The Journal of Religion*, 27/1 (January 1947), pp. 1–15, a companion essay to Tillich, "The

Problem of Theological Method," in ibid., pp. 16–26, which includes a penetrating discussion of Tillich's differences with neoorthodoxy.

Among the more recent discussions of the theological task are George A. Lindbeck, *The Nature of Doctrine: Religion and Theology in a Postliberal Age* (Philadelphia: Westminster, 1984), an important modern study emphasizing the function of doctrinal statements and their necessary cultural relatedness; Robin Gill, *Theology and Social Structure* (London: Mowbrays, 1977); Charles A. M. Hall, *The Common Quest: Theology and the Search for Truth* (Philadelphia: Westminster, 1965); Walter Kasper, *The Methods of Dogmatic Theology* (New York: Paulist Press, 1969); F. G. Healey, ed., *What Theologians Do* (Grand Rapids: Eerdmans, 1971); René Latourelle and Gerald O'Collins, eds., *Problems and Perspectives of Fundamental Theology*, trans. Matthew J. O'Connell (New York: Paulist Press, 1982), a significant Roman Catholic work that deals both with the contemporary emphasis on Christology as a fundamental issue and with the foundational character of hermeneutics.

INDEX OF MODERN AUTHORS AND TITLES

(Full bibliographical information may be found in the first reference to individual works. Virtually all the page references are to the footnotes.)

INDEX OF SUBJECTS

INDEX OF BIBLICAL PASSAGES